The Ultimate Audition Book
for Teens Volume IV
111 One-Minute Monologues

A Smith and Kraus Book
Published by Smith and Kraus, Inc.
177 Lyme Road, Hanover, NH 03755
www.smithkraus.com

First Edition: November 2002
Manufactured in the United States of America
9 8 7 6 5

Cover and text design by Julia Gignoux, Freedom Hill Design

Library of Congress Cataloging-in-Publication Data
Lamedman, Debbie.
The ultimate audition book for teens IV : 111 one-minute monologues /
by Debbie Lamedman —1st ed.
ISBN 978-1-57525-353-4 (vol. 4)
Summary: A collection of 111 original monologues, all about one minute long, to be
used by male and female teenage actors in auditions.
1. Monologues. 2. Acting. 3. Auditions.
[1. Monologues. 2. Acting—Auditions.] I. Title. II. Young actors series.
PN2080.L36 2003
812'.6—dc21
2002030413

The Ultimate Audition Book for Teens VOLUME IV

• • •

111 One-Minute Monologues

Debbie Lamedman

YOUNG ACTORS SERIES

A Smith and Kraus Book

ACKNOWLEDGMENTS

I must offer a very special thanks to Janet Milstein. She provided inspiration and encouragement and really helped pave the way to my writing this book. I extend my heartfelt thanks to her!

To my nephews Jordan Kelley and Max Kelley, who constantly delight and inspire me every day. They deserve a great deal of thanks for helping me work out the kinks in many of the pieces and providing constant support and unconditional love—you guys are the best!

To Eric Romm, who was the source and inspiration for "The Shopping Trip," one of my favorite monologues in this book.

To my family, who taught me to believe in my abilities and to always be willing to take chances, I love you all very much.

And finally I would like to thank my students, both past and present, who continually inspire and surprise me. It's been an amazing journey guiding these young actors and watching them bloom and grow into disciplined, imaginative, and unique artists. I hope you all learn as much from me as I have learned from you!

CONTENTS

Introduction vii

Female Monologues

Comedy 1
Drama 31

Male Monologues

Comedy 59
Drama 89

Introduction

I have to tell you about the time I was preparing for a very important audition. I needed the perfect monologue, one that could really show off my acting skills as well as my personality. I searched for weeks! Stacks of plays and monologue books lined my bedroom floor as I went through the painstaking task of hunting down that flawless yet elusive piece.

Well I finally found it. When I did, it was one in the morning and I was so excited I had to call my acting coach, (who, by the way wasn't too thrilled because of the hour, but was happy for me!). It was everything I had been looking for in a monologue. It reflected my own feelings about the given situation, it had humor and warmth, and it truly was a perfect fit.

A monologue is like a suit of clothing. It really needs to fit you, the actor. Choosing a monologue is a very personal thing because you have to be comfortable with the material. If you only have one minute to make a good first impression, it's certainly very important to feel as comfortable and as a confident as you can with your chosen piece.

As I began to work with more and more teenage actors, I realized there was a lack of diverse and interesting pieces for this particular age group. More and more, it seems, agents want to see a monologue as an audition piece. Regional theater companies have always required monologues for their auditions, and so the perfect monologue is in demand. Consequently, if there are a few really good pieces floating around, they're constantly used and done to death. Another important fact to remember in the actor's quest for the perfect monologue is to find one that hasn't been used by every actor in that age group. The people doing the auditioning want to see something new and different.

So here is my contribution to the cause! One hundred and eleven new monologues written specifically for the thirteen- to nineteen-year-old actor. I hope those of you who use this book will find what you've been looking for. Something new and original; pieces that hopefully will reflect your own feelings and emotions, desires, and grievances.

I have written monologues for both male and female actors and have organized the pieces into comedic and dramatic categories. As you go through the book, you will notice that not all the monologues are gender specific, and if you relate to one particular piece, male or female, by all means you should use it!

I feel strongly that monologues should be thought of as dialogues. These monologues are not Shakespeare soliloquies where you are on stage talking to yourself. The characters in these pieces are always talking to another person right then and there, in that exact moment. All these pieces are active because they are happening in the here and now, rather than memory monologues where the character is reminiscing about something that happened to him or her a while ago. Consequently, you will see the direction *Beat* used quite frequently in the following pieces. Different coaches have different definitions for this word, but for the purposes of this book, it determines when the other character is speaking.

I hope this book provides you with not one but several different pieces for you to build a strong and diverse repertoire. Whatever your needs, remember to choose pieces that fit you like a good pair of jeans. Stay honest and truthful to the given circumstances, make strong and interesting character choices, and perhaps, most important, have fun and knock 'em dead!

Debbie Lamedman

Female Monologues

. . .

COMEDY

GROUNDED

MELISSA has been grounded and is not allowed to go out for a month. Her friend Jenna has called on the telephone. MELISSA is whispering because she doesn't want her parents to know she's talking to anyone.

MELISSA: *(Diving for the phone so the ringing won't attract attention.)* Hello? I can't talk to you right now, Jenna. Because if my parents hear me talking to you they'll kill me. I'm already grounded for the rest of my life. Okay, I'm exaggerating. One month. But it might as well be forever. I'm missing out on some great parties. And J.J. asked me if I wanted to go to that concert next weekend, and there's no chance. I didn't even really do anything wrong. Just a couple of minor incidents. Okay, so that one thing wasn't so minor, but it's not like I got arrested or anything. I thought, at least, my mother would understand. But she's the one who insisted on the one-month prison sentence. They wouldn't even let me watch television last night. I had to read. Can you believe that? *READ!* I'm losing my mind!

(She realizes she has spoken loudly and runs to the door to make sure her parents haven't heard her.)

Look, I better go. I can't afford to get into any more trouble. But try to come over in a couple of hours. After the old folks go to bed. Just knock lightly on the window. I'll sneak out and we can smoke a cigarette or something. *(Beat.)*

I know I don't smoke, but I'm feeling the need to be rebellious. So come over later, okay? And don't make any noise!

BRACE YOURSELF

KATIE has just gotten braces put on her teeth, and she is miserable. As her father tries to cheer her up, KATIE refuses to feel better about the situation.

KATIE: Don't look at me . . . and don't make me laugh . . . I look hideous. *(Beat.)*

I don't care if everyone I know has them. I care that my lips are pushed out so far I could trip over them. I care that I won't be able to eat solid food for the next two years. I care that every school picture will be of some FREAK. *(Beat.)*

What do you mean it'll be worth it? My teeth weren't so bad—it's not like I had this huge overbite or anything. I could have lived with it. You and Mom always taught me to embrace the differences—well I would have embraced my crooked teeth, if only you had let me.

But now they're going to be perfect and straight and I'm not sure all this suffering *is* worth it, Dad . . . plus I'm in a lot of pain. . . . *(Beat.)*

Well, I guess a chocolate milkshake would taste good right now—it won't involve chewing. *(Pause.)*

Okay, I'll let you buy me one . . . but don't think that's gonna put me in a good mood. I plan on being miserable for the next two years and I'm not gonna smile until these things are off and my teeth are no longer being held hostage. *(Pause.)*

And Dad . . . you say one day I'll thank you, but we'll just see about that. If that day comes . . . I'll buy *you* a milkshake.

BOREDOM

DIERDRE is talking with her friend as they try to decide what they can do to cure their boredom.

DIERDRE: I am so bored! Aren't you bored? What do you want to do? *(Beat.)*

Believe it or not, I'm sick of going to the mall. Although I really do need to get a new pair of shoes to go with those pants I bought last week. But I'm sick of the same old thing, the same old stores, the same old food at the food court, *and* the same old stupid guys making the same old dumb comments when we walk by. We need to come up with something more exciting than just going to the mall or going to the movies. *(Beat.)*

Maybe we should start training to become athletes. Triathletes. Ya know, swim, run, bike? If we did that, we would be in fantastic shape, we'd win money and prizes, maybe even scholarships to college, and we would be so busy training all the time, we'd never be bored again! *(Pause.)*

Of course, training like that takes serious commitment, years of work, and total discipline. We'd never have time to do anything else. We'd never see our friends or be able to eat what we wanted or go to parties. It would be a constant drag . . . our whole life would be reduced to swimming, running, and biking.

(Pause as she reflects what life would be like as a triathlete.)
So . . . do you want to go to the mall?

A WHIRLWIND ROMANCE

CARLY is on her very first date with Peter. They have gone to an amusement park for the day. Eager to make a good impression, CARLY tries to suppress the fact that the rides and the food have made her a bit ill.

CARLY: I'm having a great time, Peter. Seriously, this is the best date I've ever been on. Okay, well now I guess I'll admit this is the *only* date I've ever been on. Yeah.

It's not that I haven't been asked . . . of course I've been asked before . . . it's just I've always been too busy with other stuff, ya know. But this is great—that last ride was amazing. I think I left my stomach back there. I don't usually go on roller coasters because they usually make me feel weird, but I'm feeling okay. *(Beat.)*

I do? I look gray? Well, I guess my stomach is feeling a little queasy. Maybe I should sit down . . . but just for a minute . . . then we'll be off again. *(Beat.)*

Oh, you want to ride that mammoth coaster on the other side of the park? Um . . . sure . . . I'm up for it . . . I think. I just feel . . . I don't know . . . a little dizzy or something. Must have been that corndog I ate for lunch. I don't usually eat corndogs, but you were having one and it looked pretty good so . . . um . . . Peter . . . could you excuse me for a second? I just want to go to the bathroom. Splash some cold water on my face. *(Beat.)*

No, no! I'm all right. I'll be right back. And then we'll ride the Mammoth. I think I'll feel better if I just . . . well Peter . . . I think I have to throw up. Be right back!

WRITTEN IN THE STARS

SARA loves astrology and uses it to help her friend Rachel decide who to go with to the prom.

SARA: Three guys asked you to the prom? You're kidding me? Not one poor slob asked me, but you hit the jackpot with three. Okay, who asked you? *(Beat.)*

Robbie Peters, nice. Who else? *(Beat.)*

Jim Rosemont? Oh my God, he is soooo cute. And finally? Justin Daniels. He's cool. Wow, Rach, you really did hit the jackpot. So who's the lucky guy? Who are ya gonna go with? *(Beat.)*

Well, yeah I can see your dilemma. They're all really great guys. Okay. Let me help you decide. You're a Virgo, right? Okay. Do you happen to know what the guys' birth signs are? *(Beat.)*

Oh good. Let me write this down. Robbie's a Taurus. Very cool. Jim is a Scorpio. Well, that figures. And Justin is an Aquarius. Okay. Well this will makes things very easy. As a Virgo you're totally attracted to Scorpio Jim. And who wouldn't be? That boy is *hot!* But it's totally a physical attraction and in the long run you won't get along and you'll be fighting all the time, so I wouldn't go with Jim. Now Justin is also very attractive, but his Aquarian tendencies cause him to be a bit bossy and he will totally underestimate you and your inner strength. So ixnay on Justin. Which leaves us with Robbie. To be honest, I think he is your perfect match. He's sweet and caring and quite the gentleman. Being a Taurus makes him a little stubborn, but you'll know how to handle him. So that's your answer! You'll go to the prom with Robbie, and I also predict that you guys will have a long-lasting relationship and possible marriage. Isn't this exciting? It's all written in the stars. *(Pause.)*

Now I just wish the stars would send a little action my way. Hey, when you tell Justin and Jim you can't go with them, maybe you could mention my name . . . As an Aries, I would be the perfect date for either one of them.

FRIED

MAUREEN *has just returned from spending the entire day at the beach. She has been wearing a very skimpy suit and nothing else—including no suntan lotion. Now she is suffering from the effects of an extremely painful, full-body sunburn. Here, she shares her pain with her best friend.*

MAUREEN: I can't move. I can't breathe. I can't even sit down. Why did you let me do this to myself? *(Beat.)*

Well I think you could take a *little* responsibility. You could have said, "Hey Mo, let me rub some lotion on you—you look a little pink."

But you didn't say a word and now I am *so* fried it isn't even funny. So stop laughing!

I'm serious I can't move! I have to walk like a tin soldier. *(Beat.)*

I guess I wasn't paying attention because I thought that cute guy was flirting with me. Now I see he wasn't flirting at all— he was staring at the whitest girl he'd ever seen!

I should never go to the beach—I can't be in the sun—I don't ever tan—and now I look like a tomato. And in a week it's gonna be even worse because I'll start to peel and I'll look like a leper. Oh why am I so stupid, why? *(She slaps herself on the leg in frustration and causes herself pain.)*

Oh . . . ow, ow, ow, ow, ow, ouch!!!! See! I can't even get emotional! Everything hurts. Every inch of my body hurts. Even the tip of my nose. Even in between my toes for God's sake!

(Pause—she hesitates as she decides what to do and how to make herself comfortable.)

I guess I'll go try to sleep in a bathtub filled with ice water. That should feel pretty good, don't you think? I'm gonna stay in there for a while too. I think I'll stay in there until next winter. Hopefully, I'll feel better by then.

OFF THE RACK

TARYN *and her friend Tracy have gone shopping at an exclusive designer shop. The salesgirl has been watching them suspiciously, but* TARYN *decides to try some clothes on. Here, she is stuck in the dressing room having had some particular problems with a certain article of clothing. She whispers to Tracy through the door of the dressing room.*

TARYN: *(Whispering.)* Tracy . . . are you out there? Okay, good. Is the salesgirl looking over here? Well, you gotta distract her so I can put this dress back. It went over my head fine, I thought it fit—but the top part was a little tight and when I tried to take it off—Trace . . . it got stuck!! So I tugged and tugged and now it's . . . well it kind of exploded off my body. *(Beat.)*

No! Don't come in—don't call any attention to yourself or to me. I have to get the dress back on the rack before she sees it. *(Beat.)*

Is it bad? *(Looking down at the dress.)* Uh . . . yeah—it's pretty bad—it's sort of split in two. I guess if worse comes to worse I can buy it. It was on the clearance rack. Let's see . . . the tag says it's . . . *(Total panic.)*

Oh my God, Tracy—it's four hundred dollars!! On clearance!! I am DEAD!! Please go distract that woman— *(Beat.)*

I don't know what you should say. Just keep her busy. Ask annoying questions. You do that really well. *(Beat.)*

Oh please, this is not the time to get insulted—just *go!* I'll meet you outside as soon as I peel this thing off and get it back on the rack.

I can't believe they would charge four hundred dollars for a dress that isn't even sewn well. God, please let me get away with this. And I promise I'll never look at Gucci again.

DENTAL PHOBIA

KELLEY is entering the waiting room of her dentist's office. She is extremely nervous about her upcoming appointment and immediately starts chattering away to another patient to alleviate her tension.

KELLEY: Excuse me, is someone sitting here? Thanks. I need to sit in this particular chair in this exact location. I'm a little superstitious when I come here, and this chair has always been good luck for me. So, what are you here for? *(Beat.)*

Just a teeth cleaning? Lucky you. I mean that's so simple. So painless. No. I'm here for a root canal. A good, old-fashioned, screw the nails in your mouth root canal.*(Beat.)*

Never had one? Lucky you. See, they have to do the procedure in several parts. They started it last week and I think he's gonna finish today. I'm not usually this nervous, but I have a particular phobia about dentists. The problem is I hate them. This one dentist I had when I was a little girl, his name was Dr. Phillips? Anyway, he pretended to be all nice and sweet, and one day he looked in my mouth and discovered my two bottom middle teeth were loose. He says, "Oh . . . what have we here?" and before I knew what was happening, he just *rips* them out of my mouth. I heard the sound. RIPPP! So ever since, I can't stand dentists. And now—this root canal. Dr. Meyers is okay, but I've gotta watch him all the time. I'm just thinking any second he's gonna start ripping. That's why I have to sit in this chair. Every time I come here, this is where I sit, and so far he hasn't hurt me too bad. *(Beat.)*

Oh, is that you they just called in? Well, good luck with your cleaning. Hope there's no teeth ripping involved. Just pray you never have to have a root canal.

WAXED OFF

STEPHANIE *has accidentally removed her eyebrows by using a product she purchased through an infomercial. She is in a state of panic because her date is going to show up very shortly. She tries to elicit some help from a friend.*

STEPHANIE: God, I'm so stupid. I read the instructions—I did everything right. I don't understand how this happened. Is there anything you can do to fix it? Michael is picking me up in less than an hour. *(Beat.)*

I already *tried* eyebrow pencil. It made me look like a clown. Do you think he'll notice? Of course he'll notice. I have NO EYEBROWS!!

Maybe I could wear sunglasses all night. The really, really big ones that cover the entire eye. *(Beat.)*

What do you think I was trying to do? I was *trying* to save myself some money and wax them myself. That infomercial made it look so easy. The woman on the box looks so happy. See . . . it's like she's saying, "Here I am, so happy, so beautiful . . . I can wax my own eyebrows."

You've got to help me. He's never going to want to go out with me again. I look like an alien! How did I get myself into this situation? Oh God . . . do you think they'll grow back?

LATE

NINA follows her teacher, Mrs. Talbot, into the bathroom to persuade her to accept her late essay paper. The actress should make it clear that she is in a bathroom by looking under the stalls in search of Mrs. Talbot.

NINA: Uh . . . Mrs. Talbot? Are you in there? *(Beat.)*

Well, I'm sorry to bother you while you're . . . um . . . having a private moment? But I was just wondering . . . I know you said that the final day for all essays to be turned in was last Friday? But I was hoping you would take my paper late because I was having some computer trouble. It's a really great paper, Mrs. Talbot. I got some help from some of my friends who are really good writers, so if this one happens to look a little different then my other papers, it's because my friends helped me. It's not because I . . . ya know . . . bought it off the Internet or anything. I would never do *that!* I really did all the work. But my brother was supposed to back it up for me, and he forgot and the computer crashed and then my mom's car broke down, so that's why it's so late. *(Pause.)*

So will you accept it, Mrs. Talbot? I think you're a really great teacher, and I really want to do well in your class. It's like my favorite class, and you're like my favorite teacher, and I'm not just saying that to suck up to you, Mrs. Talbot. I would *never* do that! I really mean it. *(Pause.)*

So what do you say, Mrs. Talbot? *(Pause.)*

Mrs. Talbot? *(Pause.)*

Mrs. Talbot? Are you okay? You've been in there an awfully long time.

THE JOB INTERVIEW

HEATHER is interviewing for her first job as a waitress at a local restaurant.

HEATHER: Well, no . . . I don't have any experience, but how hard could it possibly be, right? You take an order—when it's ready you bring it to them. I do that all the time at home. My family is constantly ordering me to bring them things. *(Beat.)*

Tray service? You mean carrying food out on one of those big trays? *(Pause.)*

Yeah! I could do that. I'm really strong. I may not look it, but I did five chin-ups for the physical fitness test at school—that's like a record. *(Beat.)*

You want to hire me? That's great! *(Beat.)*

Okay, what's my schedule? Let's see . . . well, I can't work on Friday or Saturday nights because I just got a boyfriend and well . . . ya know . . . I gotta have a social life. I really can't work weeknights because I'll have homework, and my parents wouldn't like it too much if I was working late.

(Thinking.) Um . . . Sunday is family day, so that's out. I'm finished with school by 2:30 but I'll need to eat and destress from the day, so I could probably start my shift at 3:30 or 4 and work until 6 or 6:30–7 at the absolute latest. I could work Monday, Tuesday, and Wednesday afternoons, but sometimes I have after-school activities so you'll need to be flexible. . . .

But otherwise, I'm totally available. So . . . when would you like me to start?

GOOD CREDIT

VANESSA has received a credit card in her own name and has every intention of using it—without considering the consequences of her actions.

VANESSA: Hey Lori . . . look what I got in the mail yesterday. *(Holds up the credit card.)* Look closer—it's in *my* name—not my parents. Can you believe it? *(Beat.)*

They just sent me one. Well, first they sent me an application that said I was preapproved and all I had to do was sign the thing and mail it back and just like that— *(She snaps her fingers.)* — they sent me my very own credit card. *(Beat.)*

Yeah, it is amazing—and it's got like a thousand-dollar limit on it too—something like that. *(Beat.)*

No . . . I haven't told them yet—I'll just tell them when the bill comes. I don't think they'll mind. Actually, I think they'll be grateful that I'm not gonna be asking them to buy me stuff all the time. I'll be able to take care of it myself. Soooooo . . . I am *dying* to get those new jeans we saw the other day and I want to get some boots too—they'll go great with the jeans. If you want, you can get some stuff too, and I'll just use this to pay for it—you can pay me back whenever. No rush!

This is so great! I love having my own credit card! So are you ready?

Let's go shopping!

JUST DON'T LOOK AT HIM

KIM has a crush on Neil and wants to know if he likes her. She has sent her friend Joanie over to talk to Neil and find out if he even knows her. Together with Joanie, she devises a plan that will hopefully make Neil take notice of her.

KIM: So you actually think it's possible that he likes me? What did he say exactly when you asked him about me? *(Beat.)*

Really? He said, "Uh-huh, I know her." Wow, that's so cool! He *knows* me! So what else did he say? *(Beat.)*

"I think she's in my English class?" God . . . he totally noticed! Okay, so I'm just gonna nod at him when I see him in class later. I'll catch his eye and just nod, right? I won't smile unless he smiles . . . and then I won't smile really big. I won't show teeth . . . I'll just kind of turn up the corners of my mouth . . . like an acknowledgment smile, ya know? Like I'm acknowledging his existence. But I definitely won't act like I'm interested in him. *(Beat.)*

Yeah, you're right . . . just play it very cool and maybe, just maybe if I ignore him long enough, he'll ask me out. That would be so awesome! It's gonna be so hard though, because all I can think about is him and all I want to do is look at him and this ignoring thing is going to be very challenging! But hopefully worth it!

THE CRUSH

NICOLE confronts Andrew, a guy she's admired from afar, and tells him how she feels about him.

NICOLE: My friend Janet has a zoom lens on her camera so she took your picture when you weren't looking. I got it blown up and it's hanging over my bed. I hope you don't think that's weird, but I think you're . . . gorgeous. I mean, you look like a movie star or something. *(Pause.)* Oh God, I'm totally humiliating myself, aren't I?

I don't know how I got the nerve to come talk to you, but I just couldn't stand it anymore. I had to tell you how I feel. *(Beat.)*

Yeah . . . I know I don't even know you, but I'd like to get to know you. . . . I guess what I'm trying to do is ask you out on a date. Maybe you think the guy is the one who is suppose to ask, but let's face it—you didn't even know I existed until two minutes ago so I thought I'd better make the first move. *(Beat.)*

I'm freaking you out? Why? *(Beat.)*

Oh, the picture thing? Hey, I'm harmless—look I have a crush on you—what's the big deal? You should be flattered. *(Beat.)*

I'm *not* a stalker! *(Beat.)*

Well you don't have to be such a jerk about it. I don't think I'd go out with you now even if you begged me. And you're not as good-looking as I thought you were.

(Calling after him as he walks away.) And I'm definitely taking your picture off my wall. *(Pause.)* Men!

DON'T FORGET TO FLOSS

KAREN has just come from meeting a prospective boyfriend, but little did she realize that she couldn't have made a very good first impression. When she talks to her friend Cathy, she realizes why she may never hear from this guy again.

KAREN: So I just got back from meeting Tina's cousin. He's pretty cute and we talked for a really long time, so maybe something will come of it. *(Beat.)*

What? I do? I have something stuck in my teeth? Let me have your mirror. Oh my God! I had a spinach salad for lunch and half of it is stuck in my teeth. I can't believe Tina didn't tell me. I'm gonna kill her. *(Beat.)*

No . . . it's been there the whole time . . . the entire time I was talking to Glenn there were enormous, disgusting chunks of spinach in my teeth. And I thought it was going so well too. I'm such an idiot. He was probably laughing at me the whole time. My mouth looks like a salad bar! And I had a huge thing of dental floss in my purse the whole time. If I had only known, I would've flossed right away! What do you think I should do? Should I call him and apologize? Tell him that I usually have better dental hygiene? *(Beat.)*

Really? You think I should forget it? But now for sure he'll never call. *(Beat.)*

Yeah, you're right. I'll wait and see. Maybe he'll understand and he will call. He knows I just finished eating lunch because we talked about food and stuff.

(Suddenly realizing something.) Oh my God, that's why he kept asking me about what kind of food I like . . . I thought he was trying to pick a restaurant for our first date, but he was trying to figure out what was stuck in between my teeth. Well, I guess I can forget about hearing from him. Unless he decides to recommend a good dentist.

LIFELINE TO THE OUTSIDE WORLD

PAULA is trying to defend her use of her cell phone during class time. She explains to her teacher how vital the cell phone is to her very existence.

PAULA: Mr. Denton, you can't take my cell phone away. It's my lifeline to the outside world. I'm sorry it rang in your class, I really am. I usually have it turned off, but then I always turn it on at lunchtime, and since your class is the first one after lunch, I forgot to turn it off. I'm so sorry. I won't ever let it happen again. But I really can't help that I'm a very busy person, and I really need to have it with me at all times. *(Beat.)*

Really? You'll let me off with just a warning? Oh thanks, Mr. Denton, you're the best! And I really promise to keep it off when I'm in your class. Except if there's a real emergency going on or if I know there are people that *must* get hold of me between 1:30 and 2:20 in the afternoon, then I'll just put it on vibrate so the ring won't interrupt your class. But if you see me sneak quietly out the door, it's because there was something urgent that I had to attend to. Please don't take it personally, Mr. Denton, but I have so much more of a life than just school. Some things just *cannot* wait!

WEIGHTY ISSUES

TARA is obsessed with her weight and is determined to lose some pounds. In her discussion with her friend, Jen, she tries to come up with viable solutions.

TARA: Ya know what I ate all day yesterday? Cheesecake and jellybeans. I'm not kidding. The more I try to eat healthy, the more I eat junk. You don't know what it's like, Jen. You've always been able to eat anything you wanted and still be thin. And guys *like* the way you look. And clothes look great on you. But I'm this blimp. *(Pause as she thinks about what she wants to do.)* Can you help me, Jen? I mean, we're together *all* the time so just don't let me eat anything that's bad, okay? *(Getting on a roll.)* Yeah . . . you can be my own personal food police! Oh, this is such a great idea! Just make sure that whenever you see me eating anything— it isn't a doughnut or candy or something bad. And if I *am* eating something bad, just take it away and replace it with—like— an apple or some celery. This could actually be fun. *(Beat.)*

What do you mean you don't want that responsibility? *(Beat.)*

No, I won't. I won't get mad at you. Don't you want to help me? *(Pause.)*

Oh, I see how it is— you want me to be the fat friend so you can get all the attention.

Fine. Don't help me. I can do this alone. *(Getting more and more dramatic.)* I'll just starve myself. I'll turn myself into a reed. A willow-thin model type. A size 0. *(Pause.)*

But I'll start tomorrow. So . . . if I'm gonna stop eat-ing . . . I might as well go out with a bang. What do you say we go to McDonald's and pig out. After all, it's gonna be my last meal.

THE CHATTERBOX

MEGAN has been told repeatedly by her English teacher to be quiet in class. Finally, the teacher decides MEGAN has disrupted the class one too many times with her excessive talking, so she gives her a one-hour detention after school. Here, MEGAN tries to talk her way out of the detention.

MEGAN: I *love* talking! It's my favorite thing to do. I can't help it, Mrs. Manning—I love to chat and talk about what's going on and I don't have ADD or anything—I just can't seem to help myself most of the time. If I have something to say, I want to say it, ya know?

I really don't mean to be disrespectful and interrupt you during your class. I *love* your class! And when you say something particularly interesting, which you do all the time by the way, I get really excited and I want to add my opinion and discuss the idea even more. Actually, I think talking is a good quality. I mean, what if I just sat there and never said a word? That would be awful. It's much better to be a talker than a nontalker, don't you think? I will admit that maybe I have a tendency to talk a little too much—my dad is constantly yelling at me to get off the phone, but I just have a lot to say.

So you see, Mrs. Manning, the worst thing you could possibly do is give me detention in the library. Because you have to be quiet in the library, and if I have to sit *quietly* for one hour, I think it might be hazardous to my health. I think I might explode!

PARTY GIRL

ERICA *is throwing a party while her parents are away and she is expecting her guests any minute. Here she expresses to her girlfriend Jackie how much anxiety she's experiencing being the hostess of a party she fears no one will come to.*

ERICA: No one is gonna show up, are they? Did you hear people talking? Do you know if anyone plans on coming? God, I'm such a loser. Why do I throw parties anyway? No one ever has a good time. Least of all—me! The last time I had a party the lame kids that did show up had a food fight, remember? They totally trashed the living room, and I wound up with guacamole and Dr. Pepper all over my new white pants. It was a disaster. Why didn't I remember that before? Some people aren't meant to host parties. Why didn't you talk me out of it, Jackie?

Oh God, now I really *do* hope no one shows up because I really don't want to spend the weekend getting guacamole out of my hair *and* out of the carpet. *(Beat—the doorbell rings.)*

Oh my God! There's the door. Someone's here! Let's pretend we're not here, okay? Let's forget the whole thing. *(Beat.)*

Really? It's Jeff Manning and Dave Campbell? I can't believe they came. How cool is that . . . well what are you waiting for . . . let them in, let them in. . . .

And let the party begin!

THE FACIAL

SAMANTHA *is eager to make a good impression her first day on the job. She is working at a department store beauty counter, and she's hoping to make her first sale of the day.*

SAMANTHA: Now, I have to tell you that this product is fantastic. You can *feel* it working. You can feel your pores shrinking as it dries on your face. You need to leave it on for about fifteen minutes and when you wash it off, your face will actually glow! *(Beat.)*

What's that? It's tingling. Well . . . that's . . . um . . . that's a normal reaction that some people have to certain ingredients in the cream. . . . *(Beat.)*

No . . . I don't think your face is swelling up . . . you want to take it off? Well you really should leave it on for the full fifteen min— *(Interrupts herself as she sees the customer's face start to swell.)* Oh, wow—your face does appear to be a little swollen. *(Beat.)*

Um . . . bees? You're allergic to bees? That shouldn't have anything to do with . . . *(Reading the ingredients on the jar.)* Oh gosh, there is bee pollen in here. We need to get that off your face . . . I'm not sure what to do—see this is my first day on the job, and they didn't mention anything about allergic reactions during the training seminar. Can you breathe? Should I call 911? *(Beat.)*

You're gonna be fine? Oh, thank goodness. I'm sure there's only a little pollen in here. Your face doesn't look all that bad. Honestly. And you've got that glow I was telling you about.

(Still thinking she can salvage the sale.) Maybe . . . would you still be interested in purchasing a jar? See this job is strictly commission so. . . . *(Beat.)*

Not interested? Okay. I understand. Well, take care of that face of yours. Maybe a little ice for the swelling. Come back anytime!

THE POD

PATTI has a very large pimple on her neck, which causes her imagination to run wild, speculating that it could be something alien, rather than your average, everyday zit.

PATTI: I know it's hot out. It's probably the hottest day of the year. Well, I'm wearing a turtleneck because I'm cold. Why else would I be wearing a turtleneck? *(Beat.)*

I'm sweating? Oh God, of course I'm sweating—I probably look like an idiot. The hottest day of the year and I'm wearing a turtleneck. Okay, I'll show you, but don't be grossed out. *(Beat.)*

No, it's not a hickey! I wish! I should be so lucky! No, look— *(Pulling down the turtleneck.)* —isn't it disgusting? When I look at myself in the mirror, it's like this extra appendage attached to my neck!! I look like Frankenstein! I don't know how I got it—one day I have a beautiful clear-skinned neck and the next day—BAM! Creature from another galaxy. *(Beat.)*

You think it's a pimple? This is *not* a pimple!! This isn't anywhere in the acne family. This is some weird growth—some tumor—some alien pod that's going to take over my body. *(Beat.)*

I do not watch too much of the *X-Files*. I know a pod when I see one. It's attached to my jugular vein—I can't even squeeze it 'cause I'll probably bleed to death. I'll be lying dead on the bathroom floor from trying to squeeze the alien zit right out of my body!

I've gotta go home. I have to take this shirt off—I'm dying from heat stroke. Call me later—if you can't get a hold of me, you'll know what happened. Or worse yet, if you do talk to me and I sound funny—it's probably the pod talking. Run for your life!

STAR TO BE

SHANNON is very excited after meeting a theatrical agent who gives her the idea that she is on the verge of major stardom. The thought of this type of success makes SHANNON get completely carried away with the fantasy.

SHANNON: So I went to see this agent today and guess what he told me? He said I had star quality! Isn't that fantastic! He said he had no doubt in his mind that one day I would be famous. He said I reminded him of a young Sandra Roberts. *(Pause.)*

I think maybe he meant to say a young Sandra Bullock . . . or maybe he meant a young Julia Roberts . . . but hey, what's the difference? I'm gonna be a star! *(Beat.)*

No, I didn't sign any papers, and no, he didn't say anything about sending me on any auditions. . . . I'm not exactly sure how all this works. But who cares? I'm sure he'll call me soon to tell me about my first screen test. *(Beat.)*

Don't be so negative. This *is* going to happen. And it's going to happen soon. He *really* liked me so he will be calling.

Don't you think this is incredible? I'm gonna be a movie star, and you can tell everyone you knew me when I was a nobody. Do you think I should start signing autographs now or wait until the movie premiere?

WRONG NUMBER

GINA *gets involved in a conversation with Jonathan, a guy she met accidentally dialing a wrong number. GINA decides to have some fun and make up some facts about herself, including her age and her physical appearance.*

GINA: *(On the phone.)* Hi, is Carol there? Carol? Carol Matthews? I do? Isn't this 555-1921? And there's no Carol there? Oh, sorry. I guess she gave me the wrong number. Or I copied it down wrong. Sorry. What? No, she's just a friend of a friend. I don't even know her that well. I'm sure I just wrote down the wrong number. Sorry to . . . what? Why do you want to know my name? Really? Well you sound nice too. Okay, my name's uh . . . Lindsey. Yes it is—that's my real name. What's yours? Jonathan? Oh, I like that name. So, like, what do you do Jonathan? You're a student? Really? Me too. Pre-med? Oh, so you're a college student. Wow, that's great. *(Beat.)*

No, I'm in college too. Yes, I know I sound young. Everyone tells me that, but I'm not. I'm twenty-one. My major? Uh . . . I'm a . . . well I'm not really sure yet, don't really have a major yet. Yeah, I'm undeclared, that's it.

So Jonathan, do you always talk to strangers who call with a wrong number? I'm your first? Well, thanks, I'm honored. Yeah, it would be nice to meet you too, except . . . well, you're not some sicko, are you? Of course, you wouldn't tell me if you were. Dugan's? I'm not familiar with that place. Oh, it's a bar. On Third? Oh yeah, that's a great place. Sure, sure we can meet there. Right, a nice public place just in case you're a weirdo. Okay Jonathan, Friday night, Dugan's Bar on Third. I'm five feet nine inches and I have long blonde hair. Yes, I'm serious. Ya can't miss me. Okay. See ya Friday. Bye.

(Hangs up the phone. Sighs.) Five feet nine inches with long blonde hair? Well, it was nice while it lasted.

THE STRONG SILENT TYPE

MAGGIE *has seen the man of her dreams and decides she'll do whatever it takes to get him to ask her out. Here, she asks for a friend's support but offers her a warning not too get to interested in the guy herself.*

MAGGIE: I saw my fantasy date yesterday. He works at the video store. I wasn't paying attention, and then I looked up when he said, "Next in line," and I almost peed in my pants. We *have* to go in there today and see if he's working. You're gonna die. He's a big burly guy—muscles for days. I'm not usually attracted to that type, but oh my God—wait till you see his face. And his eyes! He has the most beautiful eyes. And the most beautiful arms. Who knew muscles like that would turn me on so much? But I think he's like the strong silent type, ya know? He seemed sort of quiet and shy. *(Beat.)*

His name? I don't know, I don't think he was wearing a name tag. He might have been, but I was trying not to stare too much. I totally think I'm in love. Will you come with me? I want you to see him. And you can look, but DON'T TOUCH! *(Beat.)*

Meaning what? Meaning if he rocks your world the way he rocked mine, *too bad!* I saw him first, so make sure you back off! I'm gonna get that big burly man to ask me out! I'll even get a job there if I have to. I'm gonna get this guy to ask me out if it's the last thing I do. Because I'm serious when I tell you: I'm totally in love.

IN THE RING

JAMIE is in love with her boyfriend Danny, who is training to be a professional boxer. Unfortunately, Danny wants JAMIE to be his sparring partner when he works out and this is taking a toll on JAMIE. She decides to confront him.

JAMIE: Danny, believe me . . . I understand how important it is to you to become a pro fighter. And I support you all the way— 100 percent—I really do.

Ya know, I have to confess that I have this fantasy that you become a famous boxer and I become this famous actress and we are like this . . . ya know . . . POWER COUPLE!

(She becomes lost in the fantasy.) Our photograph is taken everywhere we go—even if it's just to the grocery store and I'm not wearing any makeup . . . which can be so annoying, but what can you do? We're famous! Anyway, it's so exciting to think about, and I really see it happening for us in the future. But Danny . . . as much as I love you and as much as I support your dream . . . I was wondering . . . if you could maybe . . . maybe find someone *else* to practice on . . . I mean *with*, practice with!

Because I know you don't mean to do it . . . and you're just caught up in the moment and all. . . .

But honey . . . this is like my third black eye this month!

And ya know . . . people . . . well, people are starting to talk!

NEW AND IMPROVED

LISA is getting ready to have breast implant surgery. Here, she discusses the benefits of plastic surgery with her friend and anticipates how her life will improve after the surgery.

LISA: So today's the day! The first day of the rest of my life as they say! I'm so excited I can barely stand it. I'm finally going to look like a woman for the first time in my life. I can't believe my parents made me wait until I was eighteen. But the wait is over! *(Beat.)*

Yeah, I guess I'm a little scared, but the pain will totally be worth it. I'm definitely gonna have a boyfriend for summer! I can't wait to go bathing-suit shopping; I'll actually have something to fill out the bathing suit with!

I just hope the doctor does a good job. You'll tell me the truth, won't you? I mean, if they look really fake or really stupid, promise you'll tell me, okay? *(Beat.)*

Well, I'll make him fix it if they come out bad. But they won't. This doctor comes highly recommended! He did almost all of my mother's friends. If he can make a forty-five-year-old woman look great, he won't have any problem with me, right? *(Beat.)*

You're the best. Thanks for being so supportive. Everyone else is saying I shouldn't do it, but they don't know what it's been like having this body. I've always looked like a boy! I can always count on you to tell me the truth. And just between you and me, if everything goes well and he does a good job, I'm thinking I might let him give me some new lips too. New boobs. New lips. Britney Spears, eat your heart out!

UP ALL NIGHT

LAUREN has been up all night studying for a test. Along with drinking a lot of coffee, she has also had an energy drink loaded with caffeine. As the caffeine starts to work, LAUREN speaks faster and faster, and becomes more and more wired. The actress should allow this to start gradually, and then increase the speed in which she talks.

LAUREN: Are you ready for this test? I was up all night studying. All night—I'm not kidding. So driving here this morning, I thought I was gonna have a wreck—I couldn't keep my eyes open, and my car kept swerving, ya know? So I stopped at 7-Eleven and got their biggest cup of java. And then I see this packet that says "Liquid Energy." The girl on the package has these bulging eyes like she's been up for forty-eight hours straight. So I suck it down, ya know? It's really gross and tastes like coffee syrup. It's really disgusting. But I think it's starting to work. Now I have all these bazillion milligrams of caffeine coursing through my veins, and I am so ready for this test, I am *so* gonna ace this test, and afterwards, if you want to, we can just skip out and go to the mall, reward ourselves, go shopping, maybe go have some lunch or something although I'm not hungry at all, must be all the caffeine, but I definitely think we should give ourselves a treat because both of us have been working so hard, and I've been studying so hard and I thought I wanted to just go home and crash after the test, but I don't feel tired at all—that stuff really works. I feel really great. *(Pause.)*

Why are you looking at me like that?*(Beat.)*

I'm not acting weird. Am I acting weird? I guess I just have a lot of energy that's all—c'mon let's go ace this test and get out of here!!

LOOKING IN THE WRONG DIRECTION

Peter's blatant staring at her chest infuriates CALLIE, an out-spoken young woman. She finally decides to confront him about it.

CALLIE: Hey Peter, I'm up here. If you're going to talk to me, try looking at *me*—not my chest! *(Beat.)*

You were too. You were staring at my chest. You always do that. What do you expect to see down there? You think my breasts are just gonna come popping out of my shirt automatically? You think they're gonna put on a little show for you? Did your mother forget to wean you and you're hungry?

I would really like to know why you have so much trouble looking me in the eye. I find it very disturbing, Peter. I find *you* disturbing!

And you wonder why you can't get a date? You're a creep, that's why. How would you like it if I stared at your crotch during our entire conversation?

Oh . . . scratch that question . . . *you'd* probably like it.

Female Monologues

• • •

DRAMA

WAITING IN LIMBO

AMY'S mother has found a lump in her breast and needs to go in for a biopsy. AMY relates the events of the last two days to her friend Teri.

AMY: This weekend was so awful. I mean, we all felt like we were in limbo. I don't know *how* Mom managed to stay so cheerful. She wanted to take me out to lunch and do some shopping—just us girls, but I couldn't pretend like everything was normal. Dad did his usual thing and hid behind the computer. He couldn't even look Mom in the eye. I guess that's just how he deals with it. It doesn't mean that he doesn't care. I guess he's scared. *I'm* petrified. And Mom . . . she's must be freaking out but she sure doesn't show it. She's going in for the test this afternoon. Aunt Lili is going with her, and then I guess we'll find out tomorrow if her lump is cancerous.

Oh God, Teri, what will I do if my Mom gets sick? Sometimes I think my Dad doesn't even know I exist . . . we never talk to each other—we've got nothing to say. Mom is everything.

I know I shouldn't worry until we absolutely know something. It could be nothing. That's what Mom keeps saying. It's probably nothing. Women get lumps all the time, and it turns out that it's nothing.

Please, God . . . let it be nothing!

MONTHLY CURSE

JODI has just gotten her first menstrual period and it has arrived during school hours. Unfortunately, she was unprepared and has stained her light-colored pants. Here, she talks to Mrs. Nolan, the school nurse, and tells her what happened.

JODI: I don't care that I got it . . . I care that everyone *knows* I got it. I mean, I was wondering when it would come. My friends were all teasing me, saying that I was gonna be a little girl forever. My mother was like, "It really is a monthly curse so enjoy yourself while you can."

Who knew that it would come on the day I decide to wear *these pants*. Why couldn't I have worn my black jeans today? If only I had gotten it this morning before I left for school, but NO! I have to get it during English. Everyone saw the stain when I walked out of the room. *Everyone!* I could hear all the guys snickering. Jerks. I can never go back in there again. Ever! I think I'm gonna need to transfer to a different school. *(Pause.)*

So can you please call my mother, Mrs. Nolan? I really want to go home. And in case you haven't noticed, I have to change my clothes. *AND* hide for a while. Like for the rest of my life.

A LITTLE RESPECT

CANDACE is fed up with being taken for granted by her friend Chelsea. She decides to let her know how she feels by calling off their so-called friendship.

CANDACE: Whenever you were bored, whenever you didn't have something better to do, you would call me. And we would go hang out at the mall or to the movies or shopping or just rent videos and we always had fun.

Now that you're dating Patrick, you never have any time for me. Suddenly I do not exist. But wonder of wonders, when Patrick has something to do with his friends and he's not around, you're all of a sudden calling me again.

You act as though nothing has changed between us. And then he calls and I become invisible again.

Well, I'm not playing second string to your boyfriend anymore, Chelsea. I'm sick of it. You only talk to me when Patrick isn't around. I never thought you were the type of girl who would treat her friends like this. How can you possibly think that boyfriends are more important than girlfriends? You're gonna get hurt. You're gonna break up with him or he's gonna break up with you, and then you'll come running to me for support and a shoulder to cry on. And I'm not gonna be there. Because when were you there for me? You have to treat your girlfriends with a little more respect. Otherwise, you're not gonna have any friends left at all. Including me.

THE BETRAYAL

SUSAN was recently at a party where she had been continually drinking alcohol, which resulted in her getting sexually attacked. Here, she confronts her friend Andrea, who she feels should have been more responsible in watching out for her.

SUSAN: Get out of my way, Andrea. I don't want to talk to you. In fact, I never want to see you again for the rest of my life. *(Beat.)*

Why? You have to ask? You honestly don't know? Then you're more of an idiot than I thought you were.

Okay. Let me spell it out for you. You are the one responsible for everything that has happened to me in the last month. How can you call yourself my friend?

That night at the party, you knew that guy was getting me drunk. You saw him pawing me and grabbing me and touching me all over. You saw me *leave* with him! Why didn't you do anything, Andrea? Why didn't you call someone for help? And then you spread rumors the next week in school that I spent the night with this mysterious stranger.

You made it sound like I was just out looking for a good time. But the truth is, Andrea, this mysterious stranger *raped* me! *(Beat.)*

Oh, don't look so shocked. I think you knew all along. I can never forgive you for not helping me, Andrea. And spreading my private life all over school. You call yourself a friend? You don't know the meaning of the word.

DENIAL

LIZ is trying to convince her mother that she does not have bulimia. The fact is that LIZ does not even recognize her own eating disorder symptoms and truly believes there is nothing wrong, when in fact there definitely is.

LIZ: I don't need any help, Mother—I'm not sick. I don't do this all the time, just every once in a while if I feel like I've overindulged or something. *(Beat.)*

I'm telling you there is nothing wrong with me . . . I can stop at anytime. You were actually the one who suggested I do it in the first place. *(Beat.)*

Yes you were—about six months ago—I thought I had food poisoning, remember? And you said, "Try to make yourself throw up, honey, you'll probably feel a lot better."

I didn't want to, but I did it anyway and you were right—I felt much better. So, every now and then if I feel like I've eaten too much, I do it. Or if I've gained a few pounds, I do it. *(Pause.)*

I'm not bulimic, Mom, if that's what you're thinking.

So you see, I don't need to go to a shrink or take any pills for depression, and if you want me to stop—fine. I'll stop. It's not a problem. It's really not. I'll just start eating better and exercising more. I really do need to lose a few pounds. But I'll do that the old-fashioned way—I'll just fast for a couple of days—that should take care of it. I can go without food for a few days. That's never been a problem for me. I can lose a quick five or seven pounds. *(Pause.)*

Now can't you see I'm fine? Will you please stop bugging me about all this?

THE CHEERLEADER

VICKI is obsessed with cheerleading, and she is a very bossy and difficult person to get along with. Because of this, Melissa, the cheerleading captain, has decided to cut her from the team. VICKI finds this decision unacceptable and confronts Melissa.

VICKI: All I ever wanted in life was to be a cheerleader. I started at four years old; can you believe it? I cheered for my brother's Little League team *and* his soccer team. I learned jumps and splits and everyone told me how good I was. I think they should put cheering into the Olympics, I really do. I mean, it's totally a competitive event. And it takes a lot of skill, hard work, and dedication. You have to give your life over to it. I train as hard as any athlete or any dancer. And I take it *very* seriously.

I understand you have to make cuts, Melissa, but it's absolutely ridiculous that you would cut me!

I'm the best you've got—I'm the *only* one who really cares about how we look out there and you know it!

If you cut me from the squad, I will sue you. I'm not kidding. My father is a lawyer and he knows what to do and I will take you to court and you will be humiliated beyond belief. The fact that you are captain of this squad is such a joke, and we both know how wrong you are for the job. You got in on a fluke. Trust me . . . I will ruin you!

Because I am a cheerleader, Melissa. I always have been, I always will be, and YOU will not be the one to kill my dream. If you do—you will be so sorry.

THE ENGLISH TEACHER

AMANDA seeks out her English teacher for help on a particular assignment and gets more attention from him then she bargained for.

AMANDA: Hi Mr. Rickman, do you have a second? I just need to ask you some questions about the essay due next Friday? *(Beat.)* Well, I can come back later if you're busy. I just have a couple of quick questions. *(Beat.)*

Do I drink coffee? Um . . . not really . . . I like mochas, ya know, but . . . *(Beat.)*

Oh . . . meet you at the coffeehouse? After school? Uh . . . yeah . . . I guess that would be okay. *(Beat.)*

Yeah, you're right. It *would* be a nice change from this place. Okay, well, I'm finished with my last class at two thirty, is that okay? *(Beat.)*

You'll meet me there by three? Okay. Then I can ask you all my dumb questions. I just want to make sure I write a good paper. That's what I want to do, you know. Be a writer. *(Beat.)*

Yeah, I'd love some extra help . . . I really want to get into a good college. *(Pause.)*

I don't want to put you on the spot or anything, but do you think I have potential, Mr. Rickman? To be a real writer I mean. *(Beat.)*

Really? Oh thanks. Thanks so much. All right then, I'll see you at three. *(Beat.)* What's that? Oh. Thanks. You . . . uh . . . you have really nice eyes too, Mr. Rickman. So, I guess I'll . . . I'll see you later.

CONFIDENCE BOOST

COURTNEY *has just come from a session with the guidance counselor at school. Here, she explains to her friend, Susie, what they talked about during the meeting.*

COURTNEY: Chapstick called me into her office—ya know—Mrs. Chapman, the guidance counselor? She said she was concerned because my grades seemed to be slipping and then she wanted to know if I was suffering from low self-esteem. Duh!! Takes a real genius to figure that out. And who talks like that? *(In "guidance counselor voice.")* "Courtney, I believe you're suffering from low self-esteem." What an idiot. *(Beat.)*

Well she talked a lot of crap, and then she asked me if there was anything about myself that I liked. Anything at all. And I realized that there really wasn't. I used to think my feet were okay, but they're really too big—and my nose isn't so hot either. I hate my eyes and I hate my lips and let's not even get started on my body. And then she goes, "Well what about your personality?" And I thought how pathetic is that—that I'm the type of girl who has to fall back on her personality because I've got nothing else going for me. I swear I walked out of there feeling even worse than when I walked in.

So what do you think I should do, Suze? Think my parents would spring for plastic surgery? *(Beat.)*

No, I don't think so either. Well, this is too big a problem to solve standing here. You got any money? Let's go eat. All this psychoanalysis is making me hungry. A cheeseburger and fries will really lift my self-esteem right now. You know my motto: When in doubt—pork out!

THE EVIL STEPMOTHER

KENDRA complains to her friend that her stepmother is sending her away for the entire summer. When her friend comes up with an alternate plan, KENDRA explains that she feels her stepmother deliberately wants to make her life miserable.

KENDRA: You're never gonna believe this but my stepmother is forcing me to go to camp this summer. *(Beat.)* I mean she's *forcing* me. She's not taking no for an answer, and she's got my dad wrapped around her finger so he'll agree to anything she says.

Next thing you know, she'll figure out a way to ship me off to boarding school. *(Beat.)*

I know, it's straight out of some fairy tale—the evil stepmother, the poor misunderstood stepchild. But what can I do? Since they got married, Dad doesn't listen to a single word I say. Not that he ever did before, but now I really don't have a chance. I'm totally screwed—there's no way out. *(Beat.)*

What's your idea? *(Beat.)*

Go with you on vacation? That would be *awesome!* Would your parents care? *(Beat.)*

Oh God, it would be a dream come true. Hawaii for three weeks. Cruella will never agree to it though. Even if your parents call her up and beg her to let me go with you, she'll say no. She wants me to be miserable. She'd die if she thought I was having more fun than her. *(Beat.)*

Yeah, it's definitely worth a try. But don't get your hopes up—she'll find a way to make it sound like a bad idea. She's pure evil, I'm telling you. This woman is ruining my life and my father hasn't the faintest idea that we can't stand each other.

MONEY TROUBLE

JOANNA usually takes care of all her own financial obligations. She's a bit short for a trip she wants to take with her friends, so she asks her mother for a small loan. Her mother is not cooperative, and JOANNA wants to find out why.

JOANNA: I'm the only one of all my friends who has a job . . . I pay for all my own stuff. So this one time I'm asking you to help me out and you say no. I don't get it. I really want to go on this ski trip with Jen and everybody and I can get the time off at the restaurant—I just need some extra money to cover all the expenses. It's not like I'm asking for a free ride—I'll pay you back, Mom. You know I will.

I've been working so hard—in school and at work. I think I deserve a break. You even said the other day that I should probably slow down so I wouldn't burn out. So I'm taking your advice. *(Beat.)*

I never get to do anything with my friends anymore, and now I have this opportunity and you won't help me. You don't even know how lucky you are to have me for a child. . . . I know so many kids who give their parents such grief. . . .

One hundred bucks . . . that's all I need . . . and I'll pay you back as soon as possible. *(Beat.)*

How can you be so heartless? *(Beat.)*

Oh God . . . I didn't realize you were having problems. *(Pause.)* Mom . . . why didn't you just tell me that you don't have the money? *(Beat.)*

No . . . it's okay. I don't have to go—there'll be other trips. It's no biggie. *Really. (Beat.)*

Mom? Do you need to borrow some money from me? I have the money I saved from the ski trip. It's not much, but maybe it'll help.

CUTTING

DAISY has been using sharp objects to cut herself. After her parents found out about it, they sent her to a rehabilitation clinic, and here she discusses what it feels like to be a cutter with her therapist.

DAISY: Have you ever had a scab on your arm or leg and you just start picking away at it, and you can't stop because you want to get all the dead skin off? It starts to hurt and maybe it even starts to bleed, but you keep doing it because in some way it feels really good. The pain actually feels good.

That's what it's like for me. That's why I cut. Because in some weird way, the pain feels good. I guess I can't fully explain it, and I suppose you think I'm insane, but somehow making these cuts, seeing the blood . . . well . . . it's a rush. It's like a drug. And I can't seem to stop. And sometimes I don't want to stop. But when people see my scars they sort of freak out . . . like my parents did. That's when I realize that what I do is kind of weird. But sometimes I feel so overwhelmed and so stressed out, and cutting is the only thing that helps me cope. It calms me down. I feel in control. *(Pause.)*

Do you understand? Or do you just think I'm crazy?

RUNNING ON EMPTY

LINDSEY'S best friend has just died due to an overdose of diet pills. Here, LINDSEY is talking to a therapist, trying to reconcile what went wrong.

LINDSEY: We only wanted to lose a couple of pounds. Nothing major. And we were told by some of the other girls that they increased your energy too. We just wanted to make the track team. We use to talk about how we never accomplished anything we set our minds to, so we made a pact that we would become really great athletes by the end of the year.

At first, the pills made me feel great. I started losing weight, and it felt like I could run forever. Melissa and I both made the team and we trained every day. We started feeling really good about ourselves. That's what's important, right? To have good self-esteem? That's what we were doing—trying to improve our self-esteem.

I stopped taking the pills because I didn't think I needed them anymore. But Missy— she started to increase the dose. She wanted to lose more weight—she said it would make her faster. It was like she was possessed. She totally changed. It never occurred to me that it was the pills. The ingredients were all natural. They were herbs, for God's sake. We didn't think we were doing *drugs!* If I thought they were dangerous, I would have gotten her to stop. I never thought they would kill her. I never thought a sixteen-year-old girl could have a heart attack. I would do anything to have Missy back. Anything. She was my best friend. We just wanted to do something to make everyone proud of us.

RANDOM SEARCH

CECILIA *comes home from to school to find her mother in her bedroom going through her drawers and personal items CECILIA is furious.*

CECILIA: Excuse me? Can I help you? What exactly are you looking for? I can't believe you're in here. *(Beat.)* You're *searching* my room? Lookit, I know this is YOUR house. You're constantly reminding me that this is YOUR house—but this is MY room. Aren't I entitled to *some* privacy? I might as well be in jail—random searches—no trust—if you want to know if I'm using drugs, why don't you just ask me? Not that I would tell you. And I definitely wouldn't tell you now. *(Pause.)*

Why would you even think to come in here in the first place? What makes you think I'm using anyway? *(Beat.)*

Yeah, I heard Mrs. Nelson found pot in Amy's room. I also heard she got hysterical and threatened to kick Amy out of the house. That's really rational. So just because Amy smokes pot, you think that's a good enough excuse to invade my privacy? Amy and I aren't even friends anymore. I never see her. I don't hang out with her. WHY DIDN'T YOU JUST ASK ME??? *(Pause.)*

So what's next, Mom? Are you gonna install cameras? Watch my every move? Do you want me to pee in a cup? Would that make you happy?

COMING OUT

TRICIA explains to her new friend Dana that she is a lesbian.

TRICIA: I know we've only been friends for like a month, but I feel like I can tell you anything. *(Beat.)*

You feel that way too? Cool. So . . . there *is* something that I've been wanting to talk to you about. . . . I just don't want you freakin' out or anything. *(Beat.)*

I don't know . . . maybe you won't freak, but there's something I want to tell you.

See . . . it's just that . . . I'm kind of gay. I mean, I'm a lesbian. Now, before you say anything I just want you to know that I'm not hitting on you—I really like you—as a friend—just as a friend . . . and I hope you don't have a problem with my being queer. There's not a lot of people in my life that I can talk to about this, and I was kind of hoping that maybe I could talk to you 'cause we get along so great and everything. *(Beat.)*

My parents? Are you kidding? My parents would die. They would curl up and die. My mother has been planning my wedding since I was like five.

No. There's no way I could tell them. Not now anyway. Eventually they'll find out, but I'll be long gone by then. *(Pause.)*

So, you're okay with this? You're not gonna bail like all my other friends? 'Cause, ya know, being gay?—it's not the only thing I am. You understand that, don't you?

FED UP

LINDA *shows up at her friend Jen's house because she can't stand to be at home where her parents are constantly fighting. She's a bit embarrassed and reluctant to ask for the favor.*

LINDA: Sorry to just show up like this—are you eating dinner? *(Beat.)*

Oh, good. Well, I was just wondering if I could stay here tonight? We've got that algebra test tomorrow and I can't study at my house. *(Beat.)*

My parents are going at it again. It doesn't stop. Just when I think it's over, they start screaming at each other again. My mother's voice is so high-pitched and hysterical I'm surprised the neighbors haven't called the cops. It sounds like she's being murdered or something.

I hate to bother you, Jen, I really do—but if I stayed there for one more minute I would have lost my mind. She's calling him an asshole and he's calling her a bitch and why don't they just get divorced already and get it over with? What are they staying together for—the kids? They have no idea how miserable they're making me, and my brother just gets stoned all the time so he doesn't have to deal with them. They don't even know their own son is a major stoner, and their daughter is on the verge of a nervous breakdown. We would all be so much better off if they just split. *(Beat.)*

Are you sure it's okay? Your mom won't mind? *(Beat.)*

Oh thanks, Jen. Thanks so much. You're a lifesaver. I'll totally help you study for that test too. Um . . . Jen . . . one more thing . . . do you suppose you could ask your mom if it's okay if I stayed here for a while. A couple of days? A week? Maybe I could just move in with you? I never want to go back to my house again. Not with *them* there.

USING

MADISON *and her friend Tish are getting stoned at* MADISON's *house. As the monologue progresses,* MADISON's *"high" should become increasingly defined.*

MADISON: Mom said if she ever found out I was smoking dope she'd have me arrested! Can you believe that bull? She wouldn't have said that if she knew how amazing this stuff is. God . . . I feel absolutely fantastic. If she knew how good this shit made you feel, she'd be asking *me* for some. *(Pause.)*

Isn't this the best, Tish? Isn't this what life is all about? To feel free and love the air we breathe and the water we drink. There's no harm in smoking a little weed. It's all natural. It comes from this great planet we call Mother Earth. *(Pause.)*

Oh God . . . I feel so alive . . . I feel so incredible. Where did you get this stuff from, Tish? I don't remember ever feeling this good before. *(Beat.)*

Wow! Are you cereal? It's *dipped* in something? In what? *(Laughing.)* Love potion number 44?

Oh man, let's go somewhere. Let's go fly somewhere. Let's go swimming. Let's go talk to all the fishies in the ocean. C'mon, Tishy, my girl . . . I want to swim and see all the creatures in the big, blue, beautiful ocean—let's go down to the beach. *(Giggling.)* I want to talk to the mermaids—c'mon, Tish . . . let's go LIVE!!

SINS OF THE FATHER

MARCI'S father walked out on MARCI and her mother two years ago. During that time, he remarried and started a new family. Now, he shows up to persuade MARCI that he wants her back in his life, and he wants her to meet her new half-sister and his wife. When MARCI refuses, her father accuses her of abandoning him.

MARCI: Now wait just a minute . . . may I remind you that you walked out on us, Dad. YOU walked out on US. Not the other way around. How can I be abandoning you when you left first? And now you show up and just because some time has passed, you think everything is fine and dandy? You think you can just waltz back into my life like nothing happened? And you expect me to meet your new wife and kid on top of that? I always thought you were insane, but now I'm sure of it. I don't know what kind of fantasy takes place in your mind, but this is the real world, Dad. I have no desire to meet your new wife; I have no desire to be big sister to your new kid; I have no desire to see you or *know* you anymore. You don't even realize how much hurt you've caused Mom and me. That's what really gets me . . . you have no idea the damage you do to people. Maybe someday I'll change my mind . . . but I doubt it. For now, I don't care if I ever see you again. As far as I'm concerned, I have no father.

NOT IMPRESSED

TIFFANY has been dating Scott for a brief period of time. When he takes her back to his house to show her his new gun, she is surprised and upset to know that he would want to own the weapon.

TIFFANY: I can't believe you, Scott. I don't get it. Why would you want a gun? Why would you *need* a gun? You're a lot different than I thought you were. I was so excited when you asked me out. I really wanted to get to know you. And then you ask me to come over here to your house, up to your room—I thought we were getting close. And now you show me this? I don't think it's cool, and I don't think you're cool because you have it. I think you're stupid. Aren't you paying attention? Don't you know how dangerous it is to have guns? You think this makes you some tough guy— some cool macho tough guy? It makes me sick to know you have this.

I don't think I want to be friends with you, Scott. I don't think I want to date you anymore. I feel really uncomfortable right now and I'd like to go home.

Guns scare me, Scott. They should scare you too. *(Beat.)*

No, I don't want to touch it. I don't want to get near it. It doesn't give me a sense of power to hold it. And you're incredibly stupid if you need a gun to make you feel like a man. A gun is never gonna turn you into a man, Scott. You've got to become one on your own. And it sure doesn't look like your headed in the right direction. *(Beat.)*

Leave me alone. Don't touch me. I'm going home.

ON-LINE

EVIE tells her friend about her upcoming date with someone she met on the Internet. As her friend warns her about the dangers of on-line dating, EVIE assures that there's nothing to be worried about.

EVIE: Don't you think I would know the difference between some pervert and a legitimate guy? Give me some credit, I'm not *that* naïve, ya know. This guy's the real deal. *(Beat.)*

I don't know how I can tell, I just can. It's the way he writes. He's honest and sensitive; he's totally a kid our age. Nobody can fake that. I wouldn't just date anyone I met off the Internet. We've been writing to each other for like six weeks. We finally decided it's time to meet. He sent me his picture and everything . . . *so* cute. *(Beat.)*

Yeah, it could be a fake photo, but it's *not!* God, you're being so negative—you should be happy for me. Happy that I finally found someone. I sent him my picture too and he told me I was beautiful. I love that! *(Beat.)*

Yes, I promise I'll be careful, but there's really nothing to worry about. We're meeting in a public place in the middle of the day—I'll be fine. *(Beat.)*

Don't you dare follow me—I'm nervous enough as it is. And don't you dare tell my mother. If she knew I was dating someone I met on-line she'd flip out. Everything will be fine. You worry way too much. *(Pause.)*

You know you should go into the chat room where I met Dennis. Maybe you'd meet a nice guy too. It wouldn't kill you to start dating too, ya know.

THE GUILTY PARTY

SADIE has to reluctantly explain to her friend Casey why she is unable to participate in any social activities.

SADIE: I'm not gonna be able to go on that ski trip with you, Casey, and I'm not going shopping with everyone this afternoon. If I tell you this I hope you won't repeat it to anyone. I'm so embarrassed I could die. But, the thing is . . . my dad lost his job. He got fired. And the reason he got fired was because he was stealing from the company. Stealing money. They call it embezzling. It's very, very serious, and there's a possibility he may go to prison. This is like a total nightmare. My father . . . a criminal in prison.

And now there's no money. I think we're gonna lose everything. The nice house, the nice cars . . . everything. My dad says he was doing it all for us—me and Mom and Jimmy. He wanted us to have nice things and feel like we fit in. I don't know whether to be angry at him or to feel sorry for him. I feel so ashamed. People are going to find out about this and it's going to be unbearable. Mom is totally freaked, and I don't know what we'll do if they cart him off to jail. It's like this is happening to someone else . . . not me. I'm wishing this was all a dream, and I'll wake up and everything will be normal again. Please, Casey . . . don't tell anyone yet. Not just yet. Let's just see what happens first. I've got to figure out a way to deal with this.

POINTLESS

AMBER's parents have sent her to a psychologist because they're afraid AMBER may be suffering from depression. Here, AMBER explains to the psychologist that there is nothing wrong with her and the entire session is pointless.

AMBER: My parents sent me here to talk to you because they think I'm depressed. But I'm not—

And I really have nothing to say and they're just wasting their money because I don't need help from some stranger. *(Beat.)*

I don't know why they think I'm depressed. Why don't you ask them? So what if I stay in my room all the time—they should be glad I'm not wandering the streets like some people I know. *(Beat.)*

Yeah, my grades have slipped a little, but so what? School's a joke and everyone knows it. What do grades really mean anyway? They don't prove how smart you are. I know some really smart people who flunk all their classes—school means nothing! It's all so stupid and pointless when you think about it—it seems to me *everything* is pointless. We run around trying to get rich and be happy and we're just going to die one day anyway, so what's the point?

And what's the point of talking to you? You can't change the world—you can't make this world a better place to live. Like I said, my parents are just wasting their money and you are wasting your time sitting here with me.

I'm not depressed. I just hate everyone and everything, but I'm not depressed. Tell my parents to save their money and leave me alone.

WHITE MAGIC

RENE has recently become involved with the Wicca religion and now calls herself a practicing witch. RENE's mother finds the whole idea quite threatening, and RENE tries to explain to her that the religion is not the evil cult she thinks it is.

RENE: First of all, you need to be better informed before you start accusing me of the worst. Yes, I am practicing a *religion* . . . I don't think you'd start flipping out if I started going to church every Sunday. Wicca is a religion just like Judaism or Christianity. *(Beat.)*

Yes it *is* a religion . . . that's what I mean . . . you think I'm worshipping Satan or something and it has nothing to do with that. I'm not walking around wearing black robes and eating eye of newt and flying on a broomstick. I'm learning to become more attuned to my environment and to appreciate all the creations of nature. Does that sound threatening to you? I'm meeting amazing people who are helping to lead me down a path where I can achieve peace, balance, and harmony in my own life. *(Beat.)*

Why do you insist on being stuck on that one issue? Yes, there is an element of magic involved, but not the kind of magic you think—nothing evil.

You have to start seeing this as a positive thing. I've finally found something that I believe I can dedicate myself to, and it makes me so happy. Don't I seem more serene and loving these days? I'm no longer "acting out" and being the wild child you complained about not so long ago.

It's not a cult. It's not dangerous. It's a way of life and I love it. Please . . . why can't you just accept this and be happy for me?

PRACTICE WHAT YOU PREACH

STELLA has been dating Perry who happens to be African-American. STELLA's mother was unaware of this and saw the two of them one day walking hand in hand. STELLA's mom confronts her about the situation and STELLA explains how she feels about Perry.

STELLA: I wasn't sneaking around, Mom . . . I didn't tell you because I was trying to avoid this very thing . . . a confrontation with you. You have to turn everything into such a big deal. I'm dating Perry. I'm not marrying him and—not that it's any of your business—but I'm *not* sleeping with him either. Not yet, anyway. So he's black . . . so what's the big deal? I thought if anyone would understand it would be you—I never thought my own mother was a bigot.

You saw us together and you immediately jumped to conclusions. You immediately stereotyped him as some "hood." Well, he's great, Mom. He's really wonderful. And he treats me with a lot of respect, which is more than I can say for some of those other creeps I've dated. You've told me my whole life not to judge a book by its cover. So practice what you preach, Mom. Don't judge Perry until you've met him. Don't be a hypocrite. *(Beat.)*

Let me invite him over for dinner. I want you to get to know him. I want you to see what I see. You should be happy for me, Mom. I really like him.

FINDING MOTHER

ANDREA is adopted and has recently located her birth mother. She now plans to meet with the woman, but ANDREA's adoptive mother feels threatened. Here, ANDREA convinces her mother that meeting her birth mother is the right and necessary thing to do.

ANDREA: Don't you get it? It's not about you . . . it's about me and finding out where *I* come from. I want to know why I look the way I do and act the way I do . . . I think it's important that I find out about those things, don't you? *(Pause.)*

I just want to meet her and talk to her. I'm not trying to replace you. I would *never* want that. *You* are my mother. And as far as I'm concerned you're the only mother I'll ever have. But this woman . . . she can tell me things about my background . . . things that even you don't know . . . and if I don't talk to her now, I'll always have these unanswered questions in my life. *(Beat.)*

Please don't be mad or upset and try to understand how important this is to me. This woman gave me life—but she also gave me up . . . don't you think I have a right to know why? *(Pause.)*

I love you Mom. You have to know that. But you also have to let me do this. You know that it's the right thing to do—and you've always taught me to do the right thing.

THE BOOTY CALL

ALLISON *wanted to surprise her college boyfriend by showing up at his dorm, but she gets a surprise of her own when she walks in on him as he's telephoning another girl and asking her to come over.*

ALLISON: Who's Sherry and why are you asking her to come over tonight? *(Beat.)*

Oh, *you're* surprised that I'm here? Well, think how I must feel. I arranged this whole weekend—my mom thinks I'm staying at Patty's house. I lied to her just so I could come up here and be with you. I wanted to surprise you because I thought you'd be happy to see me. And I walk in and hear you talking to some girl named Sherry and telling her to come over and have some fun. That was a total booty call, Jason, and you got caught red-handed. *(Beat.)*

Don't tell me how to feel, Jason. I feel humiliated. And stupid. I don't know why I thought I could trust you or why I thought you wouldn't even be tempted to date other girls. I'm such an idiot. But you're the bigger idiot, Jason, because you lied to me. You should have just told me the truth and saved us both a lot of time and grief. *(Beat.)*

No! I'm not going to stay now. And why should I? Sherry's coming over, remember? And last time I heard, three's a crowd.

COMMUNICATION BREAKDOWN

LUCY and Brian are having dinner at a restaurant when LUCY observes some of the other dining couples aren't even speaking to one another. It makes her question her own relationship with Brian, and when he appears to be oblivious to her comments she becomes quite frustrated.

LUCY: It's so sad. All around us. I see like four couples eating and not one of them is talking to the other. See those people over there? They haven't even looked at each other. They read their menus, talked to the waiter, and now they're just sitting there staring into space. And the couple over there? Same thing. It's not as if they're old and they ran out of things to say. Those people sitting over there are the same age as us. They can't *all* be fighting with each other.

Do you think that's gonna happen to us, Bri? Are we running out of things to say to each other? *(Beat.)*

Do I bore you? *(Beat.)*

Brian? Hello? Are you even listening to me? Have you heard one single word I said? *(Beat.)*

This is unbelievable. We *are* turning into our parents. Maybe we should just break up. *(Beat.)*

Oh, so that got your attention! I said maybe we should just break up because you obviously don't think what I'm saying is very interesting, and I don't want to end up like *those* people: eating together but separate. Not even making eye contact. What's the point? I'd be better off alone. *(Beat.)*

You don't even know what I'm talking about! It's times like this when I wonder why we ever got together in the first place.

UNSAFE SEX

MICHELLE *is at a health clinic and has tested positive for a particular type of STD. Here, she tells the health-care worker how she contracted the disease.*

MICHELLE: I wanted him to use a condom, but it all happened so fast. See, it was my first time, and I didn't want to seem like some whiny baby. I just let him do it. Then I found out he's the kind of guy who keeps score. Tries to get as many virgins as he can. There's a contest. I'm just a number. *(Pause.)*

I wonder if he's winning. *(Pause.)*

Anyway, I feel like a total idiot and now you're telling me I have some sort of STD? This is such a nightmare! *(Beat.)*

No! I don't have a *list* of sex partners—there was just one. He was the only one, and I only did it once. How can this possibly be happening to me? *(Pause.)*

Do I have to tell him or will you call him? Actually, I don't think anyone should tell him. If he never finds out and never does anything to treat it, then maybe one day his thing will fall off. It would serve him right. God—I would love for that to happen—it would serve the bastard right.

Male Monologues

•   •   •

COMEDY

NO MORE FRIED FOOD

JORDAN is giving advice to his brother Max about how to clear up his complexion and score dates.

JORDAN: Look, Max, it's not the end of the world. It's a zit. We're teenagers. We get zits. Yeah, I know you're going to that party tonight and Khia's gonna be there. So what?

News flash, Maxie, my boy—Khia gets zits too. She just covers 'em up so you can't tell.

If you're so worried about it, ask Mom to help you cover it up. *(Beat.)*

Stop moaning—she will *not* use makeup. There's stuff now that covers the red. Don't get your boxers in a bunch, buddy— I'm just trying to help you out. *(Beat.)*

C'mon man, don't be bummed. It's really not that bad. Maybe this'll teach you to lay off those fries. . . . *(Beat.)*

I'm not trying to sound like Mom and I am not preaching— I just know fried foods cause zits and you eat fries by the truckload. So lay off. Clear up your skin. Get a date with that Khia babe. It'll be worth it!

MUSTACHE MAN

KEVIN has come up with the perfect solution for getting a date.

KEVIN: So check it out. I was minding my own business—taking a drink from the water fountain—and I heard this group of girls talking over by one of the lockers. And one of the girls was—guess who? Mary Tanelli. Such a hottie. She was saying how much she hated high school guys and she just wanted a mature man.

Well, hello . . . *I* am one of the maturest guys I know. So I decided to look the part, ya know. Check out my upper lip. *(Beat.)*

Whatta ya mean dirt? It's called a moustache—douche bag. I figure in a week or two maybe, I'll have a full-gown moustache, and I'm definitely going to ask her out then and how could she possible turn me down? I am the very essence of maturity. I will wine her and dine her and she will be mine. *(Beat.)*

The only problem is how do you wine and dine a girl when you don't even drive?

MATH TUTOR

ELI is an excellent student but doesn't do well when it comes to talking to girls. He decides to utilize his talent as an exceptional math student to help win over Karen.

ELI: Hey Karen, I couldn't help but overhear you talking to Mr. Jeffreys about needing a tutor and uh . . . I happen to know a *great* guy who could tutor you. And it wouldn't cost you anything. It's uh . . . it's . . . me! I could tutor you.

How am I in math? I am superb in math. Math happens to be my favorite subject. Geometry is such a piece of cake. I'll have you scoring 100's on your tests in no time. You will be amazed—your friends will be amazed—your parents will be amazed—and of course—Mr. Jeffreys will be AMAZED!!

I will be doing this out of the kindness of my heart. No money needs to be exchanged. I'm doing this for the math students of America. Math continues to get a bad rap and I will make you see that math is nothing to be feared—you will begin to see the light and numbers will become your best friend! Oh . . . uh . . . sorry . . . I guess I got a little carried away there. But I really can help you—after school, weekends, anytime. *(Beat.)*

Yeah, I'm serious—you don't have to pay me.

But . . . uh . . . just one favor . . . if I tutor you and I help you pass geometry—do you think maybe . . . uh . . . maybe you'd like to go out with me? *(Beat.)*

Oh, come on . . . I'm not that much of a geek. . . .

Fine. See if I care.

(Aside.) I hope you flunk your next test.

THE SHOPPING TRIP

STEVE is at the mall with his mother who wants him to go into a Victoria's Secret lingerie store with her. STEVE is in a panic at the prospect of being seen inside a woman's intimate apparel shop.

STEVE: Mom, I am begging you. . . . I will do anything you ask. I'll clean my room every day for the next year; I'll take out the trash and not complain; I'll do my own laundry for God sakes—

Just *do not* make me go into that store with you. PLEASE!! *(Beat.)*

Why? Why?! You have to ask why? I cannot be seen in that store. If anyone sees me, recognizes me—I am a *dead* man! Don't you understand that? They'll be talking about it for years. "Hey, Stevie, saw you picking out some pretty pink panties with your mommy." Or "Hey, Stevie, didn't know you wore a thong!"

Do you really want to me to be scarred for the rest of my days? I will never live it down. They'll announce it at my high school graduation:

"Best Victoria's Secret Customer—Stephen Wallace." *(Beat.)*

You changed your mind? You're not going in? Oh thanks, Mom, really I owe ya one. Thank you thank you thank you!! *(Pause.)*

The Gap? Um . . . yeah . . . I think the Gap is cool. I can definitely be seen in the Gap. But Mom, could you walk in first and then I'll come in a little later. 'Cause if I should be seen by anyone I know . . . you get the picture, don'cha, Mom?

WASH CYCLE

ADAM *tries to explain to his sister Erin that he has acciden-tally shrunk her favorite sweater while doing the family laun-dry.*

ADAM: Hey Erin, how's it goin'? *(Beat.)*

There's nothing wrong with me—Geez, can't I even say hi to my own sister if I want to? *(Pause.)*

Listen . . . I've been meaning to tell you . . . I had a slight problem the other day when Mom asked me to do the laundry. She should never ask a man to do a woman's job and so what can you expect, right?

(He gets distracted and stops telling the story. Erin directs him to finish telling her what happened.)

Huh? Oh yeah . . . well, what happened was there was already a sweater in the machine. YOUR sweater. And I didn't notice it—I just threw a bunch of stuff in and . . . well . . . it's not really my fault that your sweater shrank to the size of a Barbie doll! You should take more responsibility and not leave your clothes laying around in the washing machine where they are very likely to shrink if they get wet! *(Beat.)*

Hey, stop yelling at me! You wouldn't have even noticed if I hadn't told you—you would have looked pretty funny wear-ing that sweater, but you wouldn't have known. *(Beat.)*

Okay, okay. I'm *sorry*. Next time I'll check first. *(Pause.)* Wait a minute! Next time YOU do the laundry. I'll do some-thing more manly—like take out the trash. *(Beat.)*

I'm not buying you a new sweater. Forget it, Erin—if you want a new sweater get Mom to buy it—it's really her fault any-way—she should have never made me do the laundry in the first place. I *hate* doing laundry. It sucks! Ya know, your shirt may have shrunk a couple of sizes, but I'm the one who has to sleep on PINK SHEETS!

NOT SO SILENT SLEEPER

EDDIE explains to his friend Trevor that Trevor's morning nap in algebra class was a little noisy as well as a little smelly.

EDDIE: You must have been really tired this morning, man, 'cause you fell asleep in class. *(Beat.)*

Yeah, well did you know that you were very entertaining? You were making a whole lot of noise. . . . *(Beat.)*

No . . . you weren't *snoring*. The noise was coming from some other body part—the opposite end if ya know what I mean. Musta been that bean burrito you ate for breakfast, but you were tootin' all over the place. *(Beat.)*

I am *not* lying—you were playin' songs, dude, and they were LOUD! Mr. Connolly was trying to ignore you, but everyone heard it—including Allison Griffin who was definitely disgusted. Forget about asking her out—I don't think she's interested in dating a guy with such an *explosive* personality!

SUPERHEROES

ANDY and his friend Ryan are having a serious discussion regarding the qualities of their favorite superheroes.

ANDY: Okay, so you say that Superman is not human. But if he's not human, then why do we call him the "Man of Steel?" We don't call him the "Alien of Steel." He's a man. A super *man.*

The thing that's confusing is that Superman isn't an *earthling*, but that doesn't mean that he can't be human. 'Cause when he lived on Krypton, he was a Kryptonian, which is sort of like an earthling . . . he didn't have any super powers on his home planet, only when he came here. The yellow sun of earth gave him powers, but when he was hangin' at home on Krypton, he was a totally regular guy, like us. His super powers make him a super human. But he's still *human.* 'Cause . . . like . . . he has feelings and crap like that. Only humans have emotions. Plus he's in love with Lois Lane. Only humans can be in love.

Do you get it? Do you understand now? He's human. *(Beat.)*

Cool. Then you agree with me. Good. Okay . . . now . . . what's going on with Batman?

PANTSED

TAYLOR plans to get revenge on the kid that caused him great humiliation by pantsing him on the soccer field in front of many spectators. Unfortunately, TAYLOR'S plan backfires.

TAYLOR: See that guy over there? Yeah, the creep in the blue shirt who's stretching? Well, last year he pantsed me on the soccer field when *I* was stretching just before a game. He pantsed me in front of the whole team, and some of the hottest girls in school saw my hairy butt. I've been dying to get him back, but I never had the chance until now. I can't stand that kid. And I'm gonna embarrass him the way he embarrassed me. Revenge is sweet. *(Beat.)*

Well, I'm just gonna wander innocently over there and make it look like I'm stretching too. And then when he least expects it, I'll streak across the field and pull down his girly little gym shorts. It'll be so sweet! Cover me, okay. Make sure coach isn't looking. Okay, here I go.

(Stretching.) Hey man, how's it going? *(Looking up.)* Where did he go?

(Looking behind him.) Hey—hey!!! What are you *doing*?

(Looking down and realizing he was pantsed again.)

Oh man!! He did it AGAIN! Okay . . . now this is truly war. Where did he go? I swear I'm gonna get that kid.

(Pulling up his pants.) Geez, that kid is good. How did he do that so fast?

MY SISTER'S CONFESSIONS

JOSH has confiscated his sister's diary and decides to read it for his own enjoyment as well as his friend Sam's. After reading it, he finds out something that he wished he hadn't.

JOSH: Check it out, Sam—I swiped my sister's diary—thought it might be good for a laugh. I read the first couple of pages but they were pretty boring—let's start at the back. That should be the most recent gossip. Hopefully, her life has gotten more interesting since she started writing in this thing.

(Reading the diary.) "The home test was positive. Now I just have to figure out who the father is."

Oh my God, Sam! Jackie's pregnant AND she's a slut. She doesn't know who the father is? Oh God, this is huge.

(Reading again.) "I think I'll keep the kid, I know I can always get Josh to help me with it and Mom and Dad will be supportive."

She's crazy! She's outta her mind! My parents are gonna freak . . . and where does she get the idea that I'd want to help raise some rug rat.

(Reading.) "And Josh—if you're reading this—none of what I wrote is true—Ha, ha. Surprise! The joke's on you! Just keep your filthy paws off my journal, you little creep." *(Pause.)*

Wow, what a relief. I mean I knew she was joking the entire time. Jackie's not that kind of girl. *(Beat.)*

I swear man . . . I knew it couldn't be true. But what I can't figure out is, how did she know I was reading her diary?

TONE OF VOICE

MATTHEW *is scheduled to sing a solo in the school concert, but he wakes up to find that his voice is no longer what it used to be. Here, he tells his choir teacher of his dilemma. Throughout the monologue, the actor should find specific places where his voice should crack.*

MATTHEW: Mrs. Kessler? I'm having a major problem. Last night at rehearsal I sounded great, right? Well, today, I can't sing a note. My voice keeps cracking. It's like I have no control over it. *(Voice cracks.)* See . . . there it goes again. I don't even know when it's gonna happen. It's like it has a mind of its own. *(Beat.)*

What? Are you kidding? You think my voice is changing? I'm becoming a man?

(Repeats in a deeper tone.) I'm becoming a man!

That's cool. That's *really* cool. But how am I gonna sing at the concert tonight? Sometimes I sound like Kermit the Frog and other times I sound like Darth Vader. I'm gonna look like an idiot. *(Beat.)*

Yeah—we can cut my solo. I guess we're gonna have to. I really wanted to sing, but I don't want to make a fool out of myself either. I'll just fake-sing all the group numbers, I guess. *(Pause.)*

Mrs. Kessler? How long does this change take exactly?

THE CHALLENGE

MAX has been mouthing off saying that he is the best skate-boarder around. Owen has called his bluff and challenges him to a match of skill. MAX realizes he has bitten off more than he can chew when he doesn't even understand what the stunt is.

MAX: Okay, Owen, I'll accept your skateboarding challenge. You may be good, but I doubt you can compete with me. I've been doing stunts since I was a baby. So what's the bet? *(Beat.)*

Twenty bucks? Really? Okay. No sweat. And what's the challenge? *(Beat.)*

Say what? Whoever pulls a varial flip to a dark slide on the first try wins the money? A varial flip to a dark slide? *(Beat.)*

Yes. Of course I know what that is. Everyone knows what that is. I can do it in my sleep. *(Beat.)*

Oh, you'd rather do a heel flip to a front side manual? Uh . . . either one . . . makes no difference to me. It's gonna be easy money.

Um . . . maybe you should go first, Owen. I think that's the fair thing to do. Or do you want to take some time to practice? Maybe we should do that. Let's go practice and meet back here in one hour, okay? And he who does not show up, forfeits. See ya in an hour, buddy.

(Pause as he watches Owen leave. Then speaks to his friend.)

Hey Gabe, do you have twenty bucks? Because I have no idea what a varial flip to the front heel manual is and there's no way I'm gonna be here when Owen gets back!

THE TRANSFORMATION

*JAY is sick and tired of his ninety-eight-pound weakling image.
He has decided to transform himself with the help of a personal
trainer, a kid in his class who successfully built his body up a
few years before.*

JAY: I gotta get a six-pack, and I gotta get it fast. Summer's coming and I don't want to spend one more year as the little wimp
who gets his ass kicked. Ya gotta help me pump up, man. I'm
so sick of looking like a little girl.

Now you *are* the man—that's why I came to you. I noticed
your transformation a couple of years back. I saw you go from
an average-looking guy to like this pumped-up Schwartzenager.
It did not go unnoticed. You are The Rock, dude. And I gotta
get me some of that. This is gonna be *my* year! I'm sick to death
of getting crammed into lockers and shoved into basketball
hoops and girls feeling sorry for me cause I'm this little wimp.
Ya gotta make me strong like you, man. I'll do whatever you
say. Put me through hell, I don't care. It'll be worth it.

THE MIRACLE CREAM

DENNIS explains to his friend how he has suddenly cleared up his complexion.

DENNIS: At first I felt like such a girl, but I figured if the stuff worked it would be worth it. And as you can see . . . it *definitely* worked! *(Beat.)*

My mom got it from some spa or something. . . . She wanted me to go with her but I said "no way—forget it." So she brings this stuff home and tells me to put in on my face every night—at night—no one will see me, right? No harm, no foul. The stuff smells like crap, and it sort of stings when you put it on, but within a week my zits were really clearing up. I know I sound like some corny infomercial, but hey—it works! It actually works.

I should sell the stuff myself. With all the pizza faces walking around at our school, I could make a fortune. And no offense . . . but I definitely think you should be my first customer.

DINNER GUEST

GREG *is having dinner at his girlfriend Cindy's house. Cindy has prepared a meal that is absolutely awful.* GREG *tries to be as polite and tactful as possible regarding Cindy's cooking because he wants to continue dating her. Keep in mind that every compliment* GREG *gives Cindy on her cooking is a lie!*

GREG: So . . . Cindy . . . this is really good. Seriously, I had no idea you were such a great cook. You could probably become a famous chef or something—that's how good you are.

I never really ate anything like this before. What do you call this dish again? *(Beat.)*

Ohhhh. "Cindy's Experiment." Ohhhhh. So, what's in it? I mean, how did you get it to be this sort of greenish gray color? *(Beat.)*

I see . . . that's your little secret . . . not gonna share the receipe with anybody. Okay. *(Beat.)*

What? Oh, no, no thanks. No seconds for me—I'm so full I couldn't eat another bite. I want to, but I ate a really big lunch, and I'm *really* stuffed. But thanks anyway. *(Beat.)*

Oh—there's dessert? Well, that's cool. I love dessert—I suppose I could make room for that. What did you make for dessert? Chocolate cake? Apple pie? *(Beat.)*

You call it "Cindy's Surprise?" Wow. It looks . . . wow . . . it's really sort of purple, isn't it? *(Pause.)*

Not too big of a piece now . . . remember, I'm really full. But it looks great. Just great. I can't wait to taste it.

MIDLIFE CRISIS

JACOB is complaining to his friend about his dad's current obsession: his new Harley-Davidson motorcycle. JACOB is ashamed of the way his father is acting and realizes he's probably having a midlife crisis.

JACOB: My dad bought a motorcycle. A Harley. *(Beat.)* No, it is not cool. It's embarrassing. He's totally having a midlife crisis. He puts on the whole costume. He puts on his leather chaps and leather jacket and boots—he's trying to look like some dude from Hell's Angels, but what he really looks like is an idiot. I was walking home with Kara and she goes, "Hey, isn't that your dad. I think that's your dad." Then he stops and says "Hey Kara, how do you like my hog." And he was flirting with her. It was disgusting. *(Beat.)*

Yeah, I suppose I'll inherit the thing eventually, though I totally doubt my mom will ever let me ride it. She has major fits every time Dad rides it. I guess she thinks he's gonna crash it, but seriously, I think he just drives around the neighborhood. I don't think he ever goes anywhere on it—I think he's too chicken to take it on the freeway—he just wants to look cool in front of the neighbors.

I swear I hope I don't get like that when I'm his age. Next thing you know, he'll be getting a tattoo that says, "Born to Be Wild." It's just so pathetic. He needs to grow up. Why didn't he just do all this crazy stuff twenty years ago when he wouldn't have looked so stupid?!

EXPENSIVE TASTE

BRIAN *is getting ready for a date and wants to look great for his girlfriend. His brother Jeff has an extensive ward-robe and has allowed* BRIAN *to borrow some of his clothes.*

BRIAN: Come on, Jeff, you said, and I quote, "You can wear anything in my closet, bro. Knock yourself out." Well, this came out of your closet, so I'm wearin' it. I've gotta look good tonight or Kimberly will kill me. It's the three-month anniversary of our first date, and she wanted the whole romantic thing, ya know . . . nice dinner . . . I gotta remember to pick up some flowers for her, too. And she specifically said, "You better look nice, Brian."

Now you're telling me there's no way I can wear this sweater? Forget it, I'm wearing it. It's Kim's favorite color, and I have to admit, I think I look pretty damn hot in it!

Why do you keep saying no, you hypocrite? *(Beat.)*

It cost you how much?

Three hundred dollars? Are you out of your mind? . . .

Who's Dolce and Banana? I've never heard of 'em . . . you are *insane* to spend three hundred bucks on this . . . what is this anyway . . . (*Reaching around to read the label.*) It's cotton! You spent three hundred dollars on some stupid designer label *cotton* sweater? Man, you are craaaaaazy!

Okay, I won't wear it. I'll probably spill spaghetti sauce all over the thing, my luck. Now what am I gonna do? *(Beat.)*

Hey, what about that black leather jacket in your closet? That looked pretty cool. Did you spend a month's rent on that too? How much? *(Beat.)*

Okay, forget it. I'm wearing my own clothes. At least if something happens to it, I know I won't go bankrupt trying to replace it!

A CONSTANT DISTRACTION

NOAH *is trying to concentrate on learning algebra, but all he can focus on is his teacher and how incredibly attracted he is to her. Here he is whispering to his friend about his dilemma.*

NOAH: How am I suppose to learn algebra when she's standing up there looking "all that"? She should not be allowed to wear clothes like that, man. You can see right down her shirt when she leans over. And the fit! She should not wear things that fit so tight! How are we supposed to concentrate? *(Beat.)*

Is she getting to you too, man? With a body like that, why is she wasting her time teaching algebra to a bunch of kids? Maybe she knows she's getting us all hot and bothered and she gets off on it. I guess I'm glad we have her instead of Mr. Lynch, who's like ninety years old—he'd totally put us to sleep for sure. But at least we'd be learning something. If I don't pass this class, I won't graduate, but I can't think clearly when she's around. Her perfume makes me dizzy, and I can't stop staring at you know what!

(Beat—then responding to a question the teacher has asked him.)

Huh? You want me to solve the problem on the board? I don't think I can do that, Miss Thompson. I guess I just don't understand it. Maybe I need extra attention. Maybe you could tutor me after school? I think that would definitely help.

TOON TIME

KENNY wonders what life would be like if he could be a cartoon character.

KENNY: Most of the time I wish I were a cartoon. Life would be so much easier, don't you think? You'd never get hurt, even if a safe fell on your head. You'd be flat for a little while, but then you'd pop right back up to three-dimensional status. Maybe you'd have birds flying around your head for a minute, but they'd eventually go away and you'd feel fine. Better than ever. *(Beat.)*

Who would I want to be? That's a good question. Well, I wouldn't mind being Spiderman because he can walk on the ceiling and that would be cool. I like Yosemite Sam. He's kind of funky, ya know? A tough little dude. And he has guns and stuff, but nobody ever get hurts when he shoots them. See, there's the beauty of being a toon. No one ever really gets hurt. *(Pause.)*

The Roadrunner. Now he is the coolest of the cool. The smartest toon there is. He *always* escapes the coyote; he always does and he always will. And he always seems so . . . I don't know . . . so pleasant I guess. He never seems bothered by the fact that the coyote is constantly trying to kill him. Yeah, I'd definitely want to be the Roadrunner. He's smart and fast, and no one can mess with him. I sure would like it if my life could be like that.

LOOK OUT BELOW

AARON is outside studying on the lawn, under a tree. When he feels something dripping on his head, he immediately blames his friend, Paul. But Paul is not responsible for the dripping. It's something higher up . . . with wings.

AARON: Dude, stop poking me in the head, I'm trying to study. *(Beat.)*

You *are* too . . . you're flicking me or something; I feel it. *(Pause.)*

I said cut it out, I'm not kidding, Paul, you're totally bugging me. *(Beat.)*

You're not? You swear? Then what's going on?

(Runs hand through his hair and then examines what he finds.) Oh God, there's something all soft and mushy in my hair. Please don't let it be what I think it is. *(Looking at his hand.)* Oh for cryin' out loud—it *is!* It's bird crap!

(Looking up.) Look—way up there. That stupid-ass bird is having stomach problems, and my head is his toilet. This is disgusting. Can you get it out of my hair, Paul? I still have two more classes left, and I can't walk around with this crap on me. *(Beat.)*

Don't be such a girl about it; just get it out with a leaf or something. I don't have time to go home; I've got a test next period. Just do it . . . *please. (Beat.)*

There's more? Oh my God, where? Geez, now it's all over my shirt. What, do I have a bull's eye on me or something? This is definitely the last time I study under a tree. Could you please help me and *get it off!!*

NO LETTUCE

DYLAN finds his hamburger inedible and wonders what is wrong with it.

DYLAN: This burger tastes like crap. Not that the food at this school ever tastes good, but this is especially crappy. It's all soggy and stuff. And something's missing. I don't know what, but they forgot to put something on here. *(Beat.)*

What? No lettuce? Why the hell would they skimp on the lettuce? It's the only ingredient that makes this thing halfway healthy. *(Beat.)*

A lettuce shortage? Are you kidding me? We're having a lettuce shortage? Oh brother, that figures. Now that there's no lettuce on here, I can actually taste how disgusting this burger really is. It's probably not even real meat. What do you think they use? Horse? Squirrel? Maybe it's coyote meat—they said we're having a coyote problem in this neighborhood! God, I'm making myself sick. I can't eat this now. I need lettuce! Gimme a buck, you got a buck? *(Beat.)*

Where am I going? Where am I going? I'm starving and I can't eat this crap. I'll go get some chips and a candy bar. That'll hold me till I get home. And tomorrow, I'm bringing in my own damn head of lettuce. I'll sell a piece to everyone who gets a sandwich for lunch. I mean we're growing kids. We need our strength. We need a good lunch. We need our veggies!

Bring on the lettuce!

THE CAR ACCIDENT

MARK has gotten into an accident with his father's car. The accident was definitely his fault, and he is petrified of what his father will do when he finds out MARK is to blame. He's determined to convince the other driver that he was not at fault, but as he becomes increasingly frazzled, he loses all sense of calm. The actor really needs to take his time building this piece so we see MARK driving himself into a frenzy.

MARK: Look, buddy—this was soooo your fault. You came outta nowhere. If you're gonna drive like that, you better watch where you're going. *(Beat.)*

Look what you did to my car! *(Beat.)*

It is *so* my car. Well, actually, it's my dad's car—but you smashed it! *(Beat.)*

Yes, you did. YOU hit ME! *(Beat.)*

Oh, I see how it's gonna be—my word against yours, right? No witnesses so it's my word against yours. Well then YOU can call my dad and explain to him what happened. *(Start building the frenzy.)*

Let's see how calm you are after talking to him, after he rips *you* a new one, after he tells *you* what a moron you are, after he makes *you* pay for all the *damn damages!* *(Transition, he tries to get a hold of himself. Beat.)*

Yeah, man, he's gonna freak and if he finds out this was my fault in any way, he'll never let me get behind the wheel of a car again.

Look, I know you don't know me at all, but I'm a good kid, and if we can just work something out here you'd be helping out the youth of America . . . the future of this country . . . that's gotta feel good, right? *(Beat. Starts getting upset again.)*

Your car has no damages at all! Can you be generous for once in your life? *(Beat.)*

Fine—report it—collect the twenty-five dollars it will cost to fix your car. And enjoy reading about my death in tomorrow's newspaper, because my father IS GOING TO KILL ME!

THE DATE

JOHNNY is interested in dating Marie. However, he is forced to deal with her brother Frank to get permission.

JOHNNY: If I knew Marie was your sister, I would never have asked her out. Nothing's wrong with her. She's great. That's why I want to go out with her. But I don't need any more enemies, so if you'd rather I didn't date her, I won't. *(Beat.)*

Wait a minute, first you get on me for wanting to take her out, and now you're on me for not wanting to? What are you trying to do, drive me crazy?

Yes. I want to take out your sister. I didn't realize I needed to ask your permission. But here goes. . . .

Frank, may I have the honor of taking out your sister Marie this Saturday night? *(Beat.)*

I solemnly swear that I am not a pervert and I will be a perfect gentleman and have her home by one. Okay . . . twelve. Eleven? Don't ya think that's kinda early for a weekend?

Okay, okay. I'll have her home by—how's eleven thirty—that's a nice compromise, right? Good. Okay. Thanks, Frank. Thanks a lot. Thanks for letting me date your sister. *(Beat.)*

(Aside.) Jeez, I'm surprised he didn't make me sign a contract. I hope he doesn't put *out* a contract—on me!

NO NEEDLES, PLEASE

SIMON wants to change his straight-laced image and be more hip. He confides to the girl at the piercing salon that making this change might not be as easy as he thought.

SIMON: Look, I know I said I wanted my eyebrow pierced, but isn't there an easier way to do this? I'm not all that thrilled with needles . . . never did too well at the doctor's office—I even refuse to get a flu shot—so let's look at some other options, shall we?

I want to change my image—I need to look more cutting edge 'cause I'm in this band now, see? Some of the other guys are pierced, and my bass player is so tattooed you can't even see skin—but I could never do that. I figure the eyebrow thing wouldn't hurt too much, but just now when you sort of pinched me there I felt a little faint. I'm no Nelly and I can handle pain, but I'm not sure I can go through with this.

Everyone I know has some part of their body pierced, and I really like the way the eyebrow piercing looks. I figured how hard could it be? I mean, women bear children for God sake, I could certainly have a little hoop in my brow.

I can't believe I'm so nervous. I mean, I really am a light-weight, huh? You're not gonna tell anybody about this, are you? I mean, this is sort of like doctor/patient privilege, right? No one is gonna hear about how nervous I was.

Okay. Be a Nike commercial. Just do it. Uh . . . yeah . . . I'm sure.

Oh God. Oh God. *(Beat.)*

Hey, that didn't hurt at all. Now how hip do I look, right?

THE BALD ONE

ISAAC tells his friend Corey that he has decided to shave his head for practical reasons and to attract women.

ISAAC: I've decided to shave my head. I figure I might as well—I'm gonna be bald sooner or later anyway. Every man in my family is bald. My dad, both my grandfathers, all my uncles. I've even noticed my brother's hair starting to thin. So I've decided why not speed up the process.

Shaved heads look cool, don't ya think? Like Mr. Clean—I'll just get a hoop earring and I'm good to go. Every single guy on the swim team shaved their heads last season, and they have to fight the girls off. Women don't care about hair anyway. . . . They like a man with a good sense of humor—my sister told me so.

So I'm gonna do it. Today is my last day with hair. Tomorrow I'll be topless . . . and the girls will come running. Just wait and see.

I'll just have to remember to start wearing sunscreen.

MISTAKEN IDENTITY

JAMES and his friends are at the mall when J.J. sees a young lady and decides to ask her out. Things are not always what they appear to be, and JAMES has a good laugh over J.J.'s poor judgment, when the "she" turns out to be a "he."

JAMES: Yo, what's up, bro. Check it out. See my boy J.J. over there? Yeah, trying to score with the hottie. She looks good, right? Yeah . . . well lemme tell you somethin'. That ain't no chick. I'm tellin' ya, I've seen him before and he sure is pretty, but he ain't no chick. Kid's name is Kevin, and as soon as he opens his mouth to talk, you know he ain't no girl. My boy J.J. is thinkin' he's gonna hook up and I am needin' a good laugh, so I didn't tell him. Oh . . . check it out . . . looks like old Kevin just told J.J. his name. Man, I wish I had a camera. Look at J.J.'s face—didn't expect that deep low voice outta such a sweet lookin' face. I'm tellin' ya, that guy Kevin is breaking hearts all over the place. We all thinkin' he's some hot chick. *(Pause. He's looking over at J.J.)*

Oh . . . J.J.'s bailin'. He's not even gonna come back over here to tell us what went down.

(Laughing.) You know he's feelin' baaaaaaad! We are sure gonna have some fun playin' with his head later on.

(Calling after him.) Hey . . . J. J. Wait up, man . . . tell us about your new girlfriend Kevin! *(Beat.)* Aw, c'mon, man . . . don't be like that. It was an honest mistake. Coulda happened to anyone. Just make sure the next chick you ask out is really a FE—male. You make sure you check her out *real* good. Otherwise, you be gettin' a *bad* reputation, bro.

A TATTOO IS FOREVER

JEFF went out on the town the night before with some of his friends. Unfortunately, the next morning, he can't seem to remember anything that went on, but he's left with a souvenir that gives him a hint of exactly what kind of night it was. Here, he talks to his friend Seth, who seems to remember what happened more than JEFF does.

JEFF: It's like a bad movie. Kid gets drunk. Kid blacks out. Kid wakes up with a tattoo he has no memory of getting! I'm not kidding— Look! It's a pretty ugly tattoo and who the hell is D.J.? Not only did I get tattooed, I got initials that I have no idea what they are! *(Beat.)*

D.J.? As in disc jockey? Really? That's what it means? How do you know? *(Beat.)*

You were there?! Then why did you let me go through with this, man? I don't want this stupid thing on my arm for the rest of my life! I don't even want to *be* a disc jockey.

Man, what the hell was I thinking?

Did I pay for this? *(Beat.)*

How much? *(Beat.)*

FIFTY! I don't even have fifty bucks! *(Beat.)*

A credit card? Oh great. That's my Dad's card. For emergencies *only!* This thing just keeps on getting better and better.

So what else did I do? What else happened? Next thing I know, you're gonna tell me we went to Vegas and I got married. *(Beat.)*

WHAT? I did what?!

AN OLDIE BUT A GOODIE

BEN is at the gym working out on the stairmaster. He sees a woman who's on the machine in front of him and becomes interested in her based solely upon her rear-view physique. He shares his admiration for her with his friend Carter.

BEN: Carter . . . pssst . . . hey Carter . . . c'mere. I want to show you somethin'. See the girl right there. *(Beat.)* Right *there!* In the purple stretchy top . . . on the stairmaster right in front of us! *(Beat.)*

Yeah, her. What a body, right? I've been checkin' her out for awhile, but I've only seen her from the back. Nice view, right? As soon as I'm done here, I'm gonna go swing by and check out the front end and maybe make my move. Watch me, my friend. Watch and learn. Nothin' better than picking up a girl at the gym. *(Pause.)*

Oh look, she's done. She's getting off the machine. I hope she doesn't leave before I get the chance to . . . *(Interrupts himself when she turns around.)*

Oh my God! Look at her! Look at that face! Can you believe it? She's like sixty years old. How can she look so good from behind and then have a face like that? That's just cruel. *(Beat.)*

I am *not* into old ladies now. You thought she was hot too . . . before you saw her face. *(Pause.)*

But Carter . . . if you block out the face and look at the rest of her . . . she's not so bad. I mean, she's got a hot bod.

(Realizes what he has just said.) Oh my God! What am I saying? She could be my grandmother. Uhhhhh . . . I'm making myself sick.

GREEN THUMB

BILLY has gotten some marijuana seeds from his friends and tries to convince his mother to let him plant them in her garden. BILLY, however, is not telling his mom what kind of seeds he wants to plant.

BILLY: Hey Mom, I was just noticing how green your garden is. Everything is really coming in great. The tomatoes look amazing, and the lettuce . . . wow! Can't wait to have a salad! You really do have a green thumb! *(Beat.)*

Well, I was wondering if maybe I could plant some stuff. Some seeds a friend of mine gave me. I wouldn't take up too much space—just a small little corner . . . just a tiny patch of ground. I just want to see if I inherited your gardening talents. *(Beat.)*

The seeds? You want to see them? Oh, well, they're nothing really . . . just a small little obscure plant that will grow, hopefully, pretty fast. I mean, it's not gonna add any color or anything to the garden . . . it's just green. Very very green and leafy. So, what do you say, Mom? Can I use some of your great soil? *(Beat.)*

Oh my God . . . how did you guess? Yeah, I *know* it's illegal, Mom, but come on, let's grow some. After all, who's gonna know?

Male Monologues

• • •

DRAMA

CONSPIRACY

EVAN'S father has just received word from the high school principal that EVAN has been caught cheating on his American history exam. EVAN tries to convince his father that he is not guilty.

EVAN: If you would just listen to me, I will explain everything. I did not cheat on that test. *(Beat.)*

Why don't you believe me? I'm your son. You're going to take some stranger's word over mine? *(Beat.)*

Mrs. Landers said what? That she found a cheat sheet? That's impossible. Dad, I swear, I'm not lying. I never made a cheat sheet in my life. I couldn't possibly write that small. And I studied. I know the material. Ask me anything. Go ahead, ask me anything about the Lincoln administration or Reconstruction or anything on American history for that matter—I STUDIED!!! I think I'm being framed. I think the cheat sheet was planted. *(Pause. A new idea comes to him.)*

I'd be willing to take the test over, Dad. To prove I didn't cheat. Could you ask Mrs. Landers if I could take the test again? Honestly, Dad . . . I want you to be proud of me . . . you've gotta believe me. I'm not a cheater.

I guess I get teased sometimes from some of the kids. 'Cause I always know the answers and stuff. Maybe they wanted to get back at me for being a know-it-all. I don't know why anyone would do this—but don't you think you know me well enough to know I wouldn't cheat on a test? Have a little faith in your own kid, Dad. Please.

THE HIT LIST

In a random check of lockers at the high school, some disturbing entries were found in TONY's private journal. Now he is on the verge of suspension for allegedly making threats to some of his fellow students.

TONY: Do you believe it man? They went rummaging through my locker. Did they find a gun? No. Did they find drugs? No. They didn't even find condoms. They didn't find nothing except my little notebook where I sometimes write stuff to myself. I write about what jerks some of the teachers are and how phony some of the girls are. Like Kirsten. She's such a tease. She'll flirt and flirt and act like she likes you, and then when you ask her out she laughs in your face and says, "I'm not interested in you that way, Tony." I told her she shouldn't treat people like that or she'd get hurt and now she's saying I threatened her. That was no threat!

So you know what they told my parents? They want to suspend me for making a hit list! A hit list! I was just writin' down my thoughts! They think I'm this warped mind ready to pop and I'm gonna start wasting my classmates.

Now my parents think I'm making pipe bombs in the basement and concocting this elaborate scheme to wipe out the school.

Everybody watches way too much television around here, man. I was just griping about some moron girl, and they think I'm some psycho killer. They're sending me to a shrink and everything. Like I'm some danger to society. Can you believe that? Me.

I didn't do anything and I'm being treated like some criminal. I'm never gonna get into college now. This isn't gonna look too great on my transcripts, ya know?

OFF THE COURT

CHRIS explains to his father that he is not interested in play-ing on the basketball team his father is coaching and he would much rather be a musician.

CHRIS: Look Dad, I don't know how to tell you this . . . so I'm just gonna say it—I think it's great that you're coaching the basketball team. I think you'll be a great coach, but . . . I don't want to be on the team. *(Beat.)*

No! it has nothing to do with you! See—that's what I'm talk-ing about. *YOU* want me to be on the team. *YOU* want me to be a great basketball player, but you never asked me what *I* want. I don't even like basketball. I'm not good at it and I prob-ably never will be. You've never asked me what I'm good at. Just because you're good at sports doesn't mean I am. And what I really want to do is study music. That's what I'm good at, Dad, and that's what I want to do.

I want to play piano—classical or jazz—any kind of music, really. I just want to get really, really good at it. I want to be the best piano player there ever was and I want to compose my own stuff and play concerts and everything . . . *(Beat.)*

C'mon Dad—don't be mad. You wouldn't be proud of a son who was lousy on the court, but think how proud you'll be when you see me playing at Carnegie Hall.

SHOE THIEF

NICOLAS *recently stole an expensive pair of sneakers. When his mother confronts him and tries to persuade him to return the shoes to the store, NICOLAS refuses.*

NICOLAS: Okay . . . yes . . . I took the shoes! I left my old pair in the box and I walked out of the store with the new ones on my feet. SO WHAT? No one even knew. No one even cares. There was no way that I could have paid for these. They cost over one hundred dollars. I don't have that kind of money and neither do you, Mom. You should be happy that I'm not asking you to pay for them. *(Beat.)*

That store isn't gonna lose any money from one pair of ripped-off shoes. Don't make me give them back, Mom . . . I *need* them. You know I do. You said so yourself the other day. And you were complaining about how expensive they were, remember? Let me keep them, Mom. I promise I'll never do it again. Just let me keep this pair, and I'll never steal another thing again. I swear! *(Pause.)*

Please Mom, don't make me turn myself in.

REMEMBERING CHARLIE

ERIC has just attended a funeral for his former friend Charlie. Charlie was an apparent victim of a drug overdose. ERIC approaches Charlie's mom to let her know he has fond memories of his old friend.

ERIC: Excuse me, Mrs. McAllister? I'm Eric. Eric Stevens. I just wanted to let you know how sorry I am. Yeah . . . yes, I knew Charlie. We were actually pretty good friends up until a year ago. We used to write stories together. Crazy detective stories. He always kept me laughing . . . he was a great guy. *(Beat.)*

No, ma'am . . . I didn't realize he had starting using drugs. I guess we just drifted apart. I stopped seeing him around school—I remember thinking he must have moved away.

I feel really bad, Mrs. McAllister. I feel like I should have checked up on him—called him up to do things—continue writing together. But I just let him fade out of my life. And now . . . I can't help but think there was something I could have done. I mean, it could have happened to me—right? I could have started hanging out with the wrong crowd, and I bet Charlie would have pulled me out of it. *(Beat.)*

Yes, you're right . . . what's done is done. I wanted to make you feel better and *you're* comforting me. If there's anything else I can do, Mrs. McAllister—you want copies of the stories we wrote together? Yeah, sure . . . I still have them. I have a bunch of them. I'll bring them over to your house this afternoon. You'll be proud to see how funny and smart Charlie was. He was a great kid. I'm so sorry for your loss. Our loss.

AN UNWANTED INVITATION

Trevor, a leader of one of the local gangs approaches PATRICK. Trevor wants PATRICK to join his gang, but PATRICK has reservations.

PATRICK: I *know* it's an honor, and I think it's really cool that you want me to become a member and everything, but I think I'm gonna pass. *(Beat.)*

It's not that at all—I'm not being a pussy . . . it's just that right now I'm really trying to get good grades and take care of my mom. And getting good grades is important to her. She's been working really hard ever since my dad split. Please, man, don't make this harder for me than it already is. We both know what being in this gang means, and I really don't want to get involved. *(Beat.)*

So, am I in trouble now because I turned you down? *(Beat.)*

Really? Because I don't care what kind of stuff you guys do . . . it's just not my thing, ya know? But I don't want to piss anybody off either. *(Beat.)*

So, we're cool? You sure? *(Beat.)*

Thanks, man. And you're sure that I won't have to watch my back, right? Because I sure wouldn't want to add that to my list of problems. That's the last thing I need to worry about, ya know what I mean?

FAKE ID

ETHAN is trying to convince his friend to purchase a fake ID and join him on a drinking binge.

ETHAN: There's this guy I know who can make these stellar fake ID's. They are primo, man. All it'll cost you is seventy-five bucks. Totally worth it, dude. *(Pause.)*

So are you in? *(Beat.)*

C'mon bro, don't be a wuss. Ray and me are getting one and we're totally gonna use it next Friday night. *(Beat.)*

It doesn't matter if we don't look twenty-one, bro—all they look at is the ID—they don't look at you. Besides, it's dark, you'll wear black and be cool, and we'll all be drinkin' brews before you know it. C'mon man —you can't be left outta this one. You have to join us on our little adventure. That bar out on the pier is smokin' and the babes are hotter than hot. *(Beat.)*

No one's gonna find out, wuss—cause like I told ya, this dude's work is awesome. So are you in or are you out? C'mon, man, you'll be so sorry if you don't come with. You'll be so sorry.

NOTHING WITH A FACE

EDMOND is a vegetarian and is disgusted by the meat his friend is enjoying. Here, he explains why he became a vegetarian in the first place.

EDMOND: That's a dead cow you're eating with a couple of strips of dead pig on the side. Did you ever stop to think that that's what you're eating? Flesh. Dead flesh. It's making me sick. The smell is making me sick, and watching you thoroughly enjoy yourself is making me sick. *(Beat.)*

Yeah, I know I used to like it, and then one day something snapped. My brother Bobby was making burgers on the grill, and he didn't season them or anything—they were just plain old burgers and they just looked like lumps of flesh lying there. I took a bite and it tasted awful—that's when it hit me that I was eating a dead cow, and now there's no way I can ever eat anything that once had a face. *(Beat.)*

I *am* not trying to turn you vegetarian, man, and don't make it sound like I'm in some weird cult or something. You should at least think about it, though. If you keep eating those burgers three times a day you're gonna have a heart attack by the time you're twenty-five. If you can't think about the dead animals you're eating, think about yourself, and what it's doing to you!

WALKING THE DOG

JACK is taking his dog for a walk when they pass a man on the street who claims that the dog has bitten him. JACK is furious because this is not the case and feels as if the man is trying to make a scene even though the dog did nothing wrong.

JACK: My dog did not bite you, mister. He growled at you and kind of sniffed your leg, but he didn't bite. *(Beat.)*

Well show me then. Show me this large gaping wound. *(Beat.)*

There's nothing there! It's not even red. *(Beat.)*

Look, I would be the first one to help you out if I thought Jonesy did something to hurt you. But I know my dog—he acts tough, but he wouldn't do anything unless he was provoked. Or if he thought I was in danger. But otherwise, he doesn't bite! He's just not that kind of dog. It's not like he's a pit bull or something. *(Beat.)*

I don't understand why you're making such a big deal over this. You think you can make some money on this or something? You want to sue me? Forget it! There's no case. There's no wound. It's your word against mine. And you're lying. We both know it. So leave me and my dog alone. You want to bully somebody, pick on someone your own size. And your own species for that matter!

LOAN SHARK

ROBERT is making a lot of money as the neighborhood drug dealer. He offers to share some of the wealth with his friend.

ROBERT: Ya know that sweet camera you saw the other day and wanted so bad? I can lend you the money for it. You can pay me back—take your time. I've got myself a nice little business. And I'm making bank. I'm not gonna ask if you're interested in my product, I know you don't usually indulge in this particular type of merchandise—but as I said, I'm willing to offer you a loan because I'm in the financial position to do so. *(Beat.)*

Hey guy, don't you worry about what is and what isn't legal. I believe in your talent as a photographer, and I want to support you. I think you should have that camera.

All I'm doing is providing a well-needed service for this particular section of suburbia. If I weren't doing it, someone else would be. Why shouldn't I be the one to benefit? And you too, for that matter? I'm eager to share the wealth. So what do you say? Ya want me to go downtown with you right now? We can pick up that camera and you can be off doing your thing by six tonight! I got the cash, baby! All you have to do is say the word.

NO SMOKING

*DANIEL, who is underage, is loitering in front of a conven-
ience store, hoping to persuade one of the customers to purchase a pack of cigarettes for him. Here, DANIEL speaks to a
man who is very reluctant to buy cigarettes for a minor.*

DANIEL: Hey, mister—Hey, buddy—Yeah, you. Are you going
in there? I thought so. Well, wouldja mind buying me a pack
of cigs? *(Beat.)*

You don't know what I'm talking about? You're kidding,
right? Cigs. *Cigarettes!* Now you understand? Great. Here—
here's five bucks—keep the change—can you just get me a pack
of Camel Lights? Yeah, Lights! I'm trying to watch my cancer
intake—ha, ha! *(Beat.)*

What? No. You're saying no? C'mon, man, you're going in
there anyway to buy *something*. It's not like I'm asking you to
go out of your way or anything. *(Beat.)*

What do you care how old I am? Can't this be your good
deed for the day? A stranger asks you for a favor—so be cool,
man, and do me this favor. You'll have good karma, ya know?
(Beat.)

Yes! I know you have to be eighteen to buy cigarettes, why
do you think I'm asking you do it for me? *(Aside, to himself.)*
Just my luck I have to ask Albert "Frickin'" Einstein.

Ya know what, man, forget it. Just forget it. I'll get my own
damn cigs. Wouldn't want to put you out or anything. It's not
like you're *saving* me, ya know. I *know* how bad they are for
ya, but I'm cuttin' down, and it wouldn't have killed you to do
this for me. *(Beat as he watches the man enter the store.)*

So thanks. Thanks for nothing! Hey—hey, buddy—wait a
minute.

Give me back my five bucks, asshole!

CONFRONTATION

Mrs. Cranston has asked KYLE to stay after class so she can talk to him about his current behavior. KYLE turns the tables on her and winds up confronting Mrs. Cranston about her particular teaching methods.

KYLE: You wanted to talk to me, Mrs. Cranston? *(Beat.)*

You think *I'm* making inappropriate remarks in class? *Me?* How can you say that? If anyone is making inappropriate remarks it's you! *(Beat.)*

Well, it just seems like you have obvious favorites in the class, and you never want to be bothered with anyone but your chosen few. If anyone else asks a question, you say stuff like, "Why ask? You're not going to do the work anyway."

You don't even try to get through to the other kids. Ask anyone. When you give your lectures, you only look at your favorite four—you don't even look at the rest of the class— it's as if we didn't even exist! And now you want to what? Give me detention or send me to the principal's office because I've been disruptive in your class. Did it ever occur to you that I'm just trying to get your attention? We're all trying to get your attention, Mrs. Cranston. Believe it or not, we're not all slackers, and some of us really want to learn. So do your job and teach us. Or I'll be asking you to go to the principal's office. To save your job!

THE NEW KID

NATHAN *has just moved to a new town and has started a new school. However, he is having a lot of trouble fitting in and adjusting to his new environment. Here, he talks to his mother about his troubles and offers some ideas about how he can avoid being "the new kid."*

NATHAN: It's so ridiculous. Back home I was more than just accepted—I was popular. I was well liked. I could understand if this were elementary school. Oooohhhh . . . check out the new kid . . . make fun of the new kid . . . but this is high school for cryin' out loud! Aren't we over all that crap? You'd think people would be a little more accepting. This school is just full of snobs. I'm serious. They're all a bunch of stuck-up creeps. Not one person talked to me today, except the teachers, of course, and they barely did except to acknowledge my presence. I said hi to a couple of kids and they looked at me as if I were some space alien or something. I hate it here, Mom. I want to go home. *(Beat.)*

No, it's not. This isn't home. Not for me. I'm not going back to that torture shack. That's what it is. You have no idea how horrible it is. And it's not like I haven't tried. I've honestly tried. But no one wants anything to do with me.

Can't we figure something out? Home schooling or maybe I'll just drop out and take the GED. *(Beat.)*

It may be a drastic measure, but I'll do anything *not* to go back there. *(Beat.)*

There must be something I can do. What kind of an education am I getting if I'm miserable 100 percent of the time?

A MEMORY LOST

BOBBY is visiting his grandfather who has Alzheimer's disease. Here, BOBBY tries to push his grandfather into remembering the details of his life.

BOBBY: Hi, Grandpa . . . it's Bobby. *(Beat.)*

Bobby, your grandson. *(Beat.)*

Annie's boy. *(Beat.)*

Right, Annie. She's your daughter. *(Beat.)* No, Annie's married now. She's married to Tom and they had a son—that's me. C'mon, Grandpa, you remember, don't you? *(Beat.)*

Yes, I guess I am a young man now . . . just got my driver's license. I have a girlfriend too. Sara. You would like her, Grandpa—she's really pretty and very nice. *(Beat.)*

Really? You want to meet her? Okay. I'll bring her next time I come to visit. *(Beat.)*

Well, when do you want me to come back? *(Beat.)*

Tomorrow? Well . . . okay. I'll come tomorrow and I'll bring Sara. Now promise me something, Grandpa. Promise me that you'll remember me tomorrow when I come back. You've got to try harder . . . try to remember as much as you can. You've had a great life, Grandpa . . . you want to remember it, don't you?

I think you can beat this lousy disease but only if you *try*. *(Beat.)*

Okay, sorry. I won't say lousy anymore . . . but you've got to make a promise to me too. I promise to use better language if you promise to work on your memory. Okay, Gramps? Do we have a deal? *(Beat.)*

It's Bobby, Grandpa. I'm Bobby.

ON THE RUN

JIMMY is nervous about talking to Rocky, a rather shady character.

JIMMY: I need to make as much money as fast as possible, bro. I'm talking large quantities of cash. I gotta get my own place, man. It's a very bad situation at home and I gotta get outta there. So . . . I thought you could hook me up, ya know? I heard you have a lot of connections with people who could use someone like me. To do an errand or two, ya know what I mean? I have no problem doing *anything*. I mean I'll do *anything*. Whatever it takes. I just gotta make bank ASAP, ya know? *(Beat.)*

So whatta ya think? Can you help me out? 'Cause if I don't get outta there by next week—someone's gonna be dead, man. I'm not kidding—things are *that* bad. Someone's gonna be dead . . . and that someone might be me. My old man's on a rampage, and I can't be around him when he goes off like that. No telling what might happen. Please buddy, I'm kinda desperate. Can you hook me up?

EMPTY SHELL

After being rejected and then accepted by one of the prettiest and most popular girls at school, JOEL now has the opportunity to tell her what he really thinks about her.

JOEL: What I don't understand is why you totally dissed me in front of your friends, and now that no one is around, you're coming on to me. You think I want to go out with you now? You're such a hypocrite. I suppose I'm not good enough for you when the other girls are around, but since we're alone I'll do. Forget it, Tina. I wanted to go out with you because, aside from being beautiful, I thought you were cool too. But now I see you're just another shallow bimbo with a great body. You're just another sheep in the crowd—following everyone else and never thinking for yourself.

Well sorry, but I'm no charity case. It would be nice to be seen on a date with you, but I'm not that desperate. I obviously don't care as much about my reputation as you do. And if going out with me would tarnish your rep, don't do me any favors. It's too bad, Tina . . . I didn't think you fit the stereotype. But obviously you do. You're the kind of person who gives beautiful women a bad name. It's all on the outside and inside there's nothin'.

DEAD MAN'S CURVE

JAKE tries to prevent his friend Cal not to drive drunk and reminds him that a similar action resulted in the death of Cal's brother only a short time ago.

JAKE: Man, are you outta your mind? Did you already forget what happened to Dylan last year? It was the same road at the same time of night, and he wrapped *his* car around a telephone pole. *(Beat.)*

Don't give me that crap! It can so happen to you and probably will considering how many beers you just drank. Don't you think Dylan thought the same thing? I'm not getting in that car with you unless you let me drive. *(Beat.)*

No—maybe you aren't completely wasted, but you're pretty buzzed and you're being a total idiot. *(Beat.)*

I'm not being a pussy, Cal; I would just like to live to see my next birthday. *(Pause.)*

Give me the keys, Cal. I don't get why you'd want to take a chance like that. Think about what it would do to your parents if anything happened to you. First Dylan, and then you— both their sons. Don't do it, man. Give me the keys.

GRAFFITI ART

CARLOS is a graffiti artist who is being questioned by the police because they think he is destroying public property by spray painting on the side of a building. CARLOS tries to explain that he is simply trying to practice his art.

CARLOS: Look sir, officer . . . sir . . . I am not a vandal. I am not defacing public property or whatever. I'm an artist, not a tagger. I'm doing my art. Can't you see the difference? This isn't graffiti! This is a painting. This neighborhood is so dingy, and I thought it could use some color. I thought I could cheer people up by painting something beautiful. And now you want to arrest me because I'm trying to do something good? *(Beat.)*

I am not mouthing off to you officer . . . sir . . . I'm trying to explain that I am not some criminal. I just want to do my art. And make the people in my neighborhood proud to live here. I didn't think what I was doing was wrong. And if you ask anybody around here, they'll tell you they like my stuff. They like seeing the murals I paint—it makes this place a little more cheerful—a little bit better. I just want to be proud of where I live, instead of ashamed. I'm just tryin' to brighten the place up—don't you understand that?

BEST FRIENDS

GAVIN and Beth are best friends, but Beth realizes she has fallen in love with GAVIN and wants more out of their relationship. GAVIN explains that he treasures Beth's friendship, but since he is gay, he cannot be intimately involved with her.

GAVIN: I know this is hard for you, Beth—believe it or not it's hard for me too. I would never do anything to hurt you or make you mad at me—I hate when you're mad at me . . . but I can't be your boyfriend and you *know* that!

I'm gay . . . I'm 100 percent homosexual and it's been hard enough dealing with that fact and coming to terms with that . . . and now you tell me you're in love with me and . . . I don't know what to say.

You're my best friend—I've never had anyone who *gets* me like you do.

I love being with you and hangin' out with you but it can never be more than that.

I love you so much . . . but . . . I . . . I . . . can't be like . . . your lover, ya know? It feels weird even talking about this—you were one of the first people I came out to, and I'll never forget when I told you I finally figured out what was up with me, you said, "I already knew you were gay. I was just waiting for you to figure it out." I mean, you knew before I did. You're amazing. *(Pause.)*

You'll find someone Beth—I know you will—and I'll be there for you in every way I can. Every way but . . . *that* way. *(Beat.)*

Please don't cry. Please don't be mad. I *need* you in my life. And we're best friends! Can't that please be enough?

SAVING A LIFE

JOEY finds his younger brother, Victor, in the garage with a gun in his mouth. Here, he tries to persuade Victor that he has a lot of things worth living for.

JOEY: Victor . . . hey, man . . . you've got a lot of things goin' for you. Mom loves you and I love you and Emily loves you . . . *(Beat.)*

She does too love you; she's just confused right now—and you have that beautiful little daughter who not only loves you, but *needs* you. You went through life without a father, don't let her go through life without one. Don't do this, Victor . . . please. Think what you will do to all of us. You'll break our hearts. *(Beat.)*

You are not a loser! You are *not* a waste of space! Hey, man, I turned it around, remember? Man, if I could do it, anyone could. I screwed up plenty . . . but now I'm goin' to school, and I'm learning that people give you a chance if you show that you're serious and want to learn. And you're NOT a screw-up, Vic. I swear, I'll help you get back on your feet. I'll help you get a job, and I'll talk to Emily if you want me to, and convince her to move back in with us. But if you do this, man, if you pull that trigger—I can't help you ever again. Ain't no second chances, man, if you use that thing. So take it out of your mouth, Victor . . . C'mon—I'm your brother, man, I'm your family—I won't let nothin' bad happen to you, if I can help it. C'mon, Vic . . . c'mon, little bro—give me the gun.

IT'S A FAMILY AFFAIR

ELLIOTT knows his father is having an affair and confronts him.

ELLIOTT: Don't lie to my face, Dad. I *saw* you with her. And don't try to tell me she was your "colleague." You don't go around kissing your colleagues on the mouth, do you? *(Beat.)*

What do I want from you? I want you to admit it . . . say the words . . . tell me you're having an affair. And then I want you to tell me why. I don't get it . . . I don't understand how you can do this to Mom—to all of us. I hope it's worth it, Dad, because you're about to ruin our entire family. Or don't you care? Now that you've got some young beautiful girl on your arm, nothing else matters. It made me sick, Dad. I wanted to throw up when I saw you with her. How old is she, by the way? She didn't look much older than me. *(Beat.)*

No, I haven't said anything to Mom. But I'm sure she knows. Haven't you noticed how unhappy she's been lately? *(Pause.)*

You make me sick. You don't care about anyone or anything except yourself and your own happiness. How can I ever trust you again? You've not only betrayed Mom; you've betrayed all of us. It's not up to me to tell Mom, you've got to tell her. And then I hope she throws you out and sues you for every last dime you have. I never thought my own father could be such a low-life scumbag. But you definitely are, Dad. You definitely are. Thanks for teaching me a valuable lesson, Dad. You can't trust anybody. Not even your own parents.

UNFAITHFUL

DAVID has found out that his girlfriend Julie cheated on him. He confronts her and tries to save the relationship.

DAVID: Julie, please don't walk away when I'm trying to talk to you. You always want to talk, so now that I'm willing, you're not. I know you went to Mickey's party last weekend when I was out of town with my parents. I don't care about that. What I care about is that I heard you left with Jake. I heard you guys were all over each other the whole time and then you left with him. *(Beat.)*

It doesn't matter who told me; I want to know if it's true. *(Beat.)*

It is? Why would you do that to me, Julie? Why would you scam me like that? *(Beat.)*

What? You're tired of us? What the hell is that supposed to mean? We're good together, Jules, you *know* that—why would you want to throw it all away? I can't believe in one weekend Jake Larson came in and swept you off your feet, and now you're willing to throw away everything we had together. I thought I knew you, Julie. And I thought I could trust you. But you turned out to be a little skank, just like the rest of your friends.

And when Jake steps out on *you* and breaks your heart—don't come running back to me.

AN UNWANTED ADMIRER

JESSE has come to praise the teacher who has helped him graduate high school. His so-called crush on her, however, is not entirely innocent and is a bit obsessive.

JESSE: Hi, Mrs. Johnson. I just wanted to come by to tell you that I hope you have a great summer vacation. And I also wanted to tell you that . . . well, I'll miss you over the summer . . . and next year too, since I won't be going here anymore. Thanks to you, I'm finally graduating!

Mrs. Johnson, I want you to know how much I appreciate everything you did for me. I mean, if it weren't for you I'd still be stuck in the tenth grade trying to read a bunch of dumb books. You really are an amazing person. And a beautiful woman too. I don't want you to take this the wrong way or anything, but I sure do envy Mr. Johnson. He must be the luckiest guy on the planet being married to you. You're so beautiful and kind and . . . *(Beat.)*

Oh, I'm sorry . . . I didn't mean to embarrass you or make you feel uncomfortable. I just wanted to thank you for everything you've done for me. And I can't help it if I find you attractive, Mrs. Johnson. But I understand if you want me to go . . . I just wish I could see you from time to time . . . just to see how you're doing and all . . . maybe take you out to dinner? *(Beat.)*

You don't think that would be appropriate? I guess I understand. Well, okay then . . . I'll go if you want me to. But thanks again for everything, Helen . . . I mean, Mrs. Johnson. I'll never forget you and everything you did for me. I think about you all the time anyway. I sure do wish I could see you again. Who knows? Maybe we'll run into each other one of these days. I sure would like that. I sure would.

GOOD SON, BAD SON

MICHAEL feels he's been ignored his whole life by his parents and shadowed by his overachieving brother, James. Here, James confronts MICHAEL about his drinking, and MICHAEL lets the truth be known.

MICHAEL: Yeah, it's true . . . I've been filching from Mom and Dad's liquor cabinet. But what's it to you? What business is it of yours? Did they say anything to you? *(Beat.)*

Oh, they think it's you? Yeah, right. Mr. Perfect straight A's I'm going to Yale next year swipes booze from Mommy and Daddy. That's rich.

So whatta ya want from me, a written confession to Mom and Dad so they let you off the hook? Forget it. It's so typical. I am so invisible in this house they don't even suspect the more likely candidate. I don't even think they realize they have two sons. God forbid your wonderful future should be disrupted if it turns out *you* have a drinking problem.

So go ahead, tell them I've been drinking their fifty-dollar Scotch—tell them I've really started developing a taste for it. I don't care if they kick me out of here—it'll be better than living with Mr. and Mrs. Brady and the Boy Wonder. *(Beat.)*

Don't start pretending now like you care, James. The only reason you're even talking to me is because you don't want to get in trouble. Always the good boy—always the good son. Ya know you should try a little of their Scotch—it might loosen you up a little.

MISSED OPPORTUNITY

After finding out all his friends are going away to college, TIM laments that he never worked hard enough in school and is now stuck working at a menial job and has no hope for the future.

TIM: Everyone is getting into their first-choice school. Everyone! You did . . . Alex did. Eddie and Jake *both* did. Kyle got in with a full athletic scholarship. I got nothin'! NOTHING! What am I suppose to do? I'm a total loser. I have no skills . . . terrible at sports . . . not smart . . . not talented. What am I suppose to do when school is over? My mom's already on my case to get a job and move out. She can't wait to be rid of me.

So I guess I'll work at 7-Eleven for the rest of my life. How exciting! I couldn't even cut it at Starbucks. Kept burning myself on that damn cappuccino machine. I hated working there anyway. The people treat you like crap. At least at 7-Eleven the customers are mostly losers too. At 2 A.M. anyway. It would be great to be able to go away to college. You're gonna have it made, man. I wish I woulda tried harder when I had the chance. You're not suppose to have regrets at eighteen, but I sure do. I totally screwed up. And I got nobody to blame but myself.

FATHER'S DAY

RAY and his sister Kim are visiting their father in the hospital. Their father walked out on them years before but recently made an attempt to reunite. Now he is very ill, and RAY explains his feelings to his sister.

RAY: The tube down his throat is what's helping him breathe. He opened his eyes slightly a couple of times, but he's never been fully awake. It's probably better that he doesn't wake up; he wouldn't be able to talk anyway. *(Pause.)*

I can't believe this is happening.

Just when he decides that he wants his kids back in his life, he goes and gets sick. We didn't get any time together. To talk and get to know each other. That's all I ever wanted, ya know? I wanted to have a relationship with my father. And I forgave him for walking out when we were kids. I was willing to let that go if we could be in each other's lives now. I feel like I'm losing him all over again. *(Beat.)*

Don't say that, Kim. Don't say it serves him right. You only heard one side of the story. Mom's side. And she was hurt and angry so she said some pretty rotten things about him. But she also told me some good stuff too. He must have had his reasons for leaving. And I just wish we could hear what they were. But the truth is, Kimmy, he's dying. And we're never gonna have another chance to get to know our father. And that really stinks, Kim. It really stinks.

ONE BIG HAPPY FAMILY

RICKY has gotten his girlfriend pregnant. He now appeals to his father for his love and support and tries to convince him they should keep the baby.

RICKY: Dad, you've always taught us to be honest, and to do the right thing. Well, that's what I'm trying to do now, Dad. So please just listen to me before you say anything. This isn't easy, but I'll just come out and say it. Emily is pregnant. She told me yesterday, and now we're trying to figure out what to do. I felt like I could talk to you, Dad. I wanted to come to you for advice. See, there's no way Emily can tell her parents. They're so strict—they'd kill her. They'd kick her out into the street.

We love each other, Dad. Her mother doesn't seem to understand kids our age are capable of these serious feelings. I want to marry her, Dad, but I'm smart enough to realize we're too young.

But we both thought maybe it would still be possible to have the baby. If you and Mom wanted to help us out—we could live here and still finish school and keep the baby. I think if we do that, Emily's parents will disown her—but if we could have your support, I know we'd be okay. You care about Emily, don't you, Dad? You said she was like a daughter to you . . . remember when you said that?

And I know I'd be a good father to this baby. After all, I learned from the best. So what do you think, Pop? Could we all just live here? One big happy family? I think we can make it work, don't you, Dad? Don't you?

THE TRUTH REVEALED

GERALD finally tells his girlfriend, Rosa, the truth about why they will never be able to sleep together.

GERALD: I do love you, Rosa, you *know* I do. But I can't sleep with you. It's not that I don't want to; believe me, I want to. It's just that I can't.

I know you said I could tell you anything, but I'm not sure you want to hear this. *(Beat.)*

Okay, I'll tell you, but please remember how much you mean to me. Well, the thing is, I'm . . . I'm HIV positive. I know I should have told you a long time ago. When we first started going out. But I didn't think things would go this far, and I never thought we'd fall in love. We started out as friends, remember? And I always thought we'd just be friends. Nothing more. Maybe I was hoping nothing more, because I knew we could never be physical.

So there it is. That's the truth and now it's out in the open. And the last thing I would ever want to do is put you at risk. I was stupid and reckless and that's how this happened to me in the first place. But I won't be irresponsible anymore, and I would die if anything ever happened to you.

I'm sorry, Rosa. I'm so sorry.

DEBBIE LAMEDMAN has been engaged in various aspects of the-aterarts for most of her life. An actress, writer, and teacher, she received her MFA from Brandeis University in theater arts perform-ance. Her extensive performing background includes working Off-Broadway and with various regional theater companies on both the east and west coasts.

Debbie is also the author of her own one-woman show, *Phat*, which she performed in both Massachusetts and New York City.

Currently living in Southern California, Debbie remains active in her field as an oral communications instructor at Brooks College in Long Beach, as a vocal coach at the Academy of Radio Broadcasting in Huntington Beach, and as a private acting coach for students and professionals, teens and adults. She recently joined the faculty at South Coast Repertory, the Tony Award–winning regional theater, where she teaches acting in the Youth Conservatory Program.

Debbie welcomes comments and feedback regarding the mono-logues and can be reached at monologs4u@aol.com.